SERVICE MANAGEMENT STRATEGIES THAT WORK: GUIDANCE FOR EXECUTIVES

Other publications by Van Haren Publishing

Van Haren Publishing (VHP) specializes in titles on Best Practices, methods and standards within IT and business management.

These publications are grouped in the following series: *ITSM Library* (on behalf of ITSMF International), *Best Practice* and *IT Management Topics*. VHP is also publisher on behalf of leading companies and institutions, eg The Open Group, IPMA-NL, CA, Getronics, Pink Elephant). At the time of going to press the following books are available:

IT (Service) Management / IT Governance

ITSM, ITIL® V3 and ITIL® V2

Foundations of IT Service Management – based on ITIL V3 (English and Dutch versions Autumn 2007, French, German, Japanese and Spanish editions: Winter 2007)
IT Service Management – An Introduction (English and Dutch versions Autumn 2007, French, German, Japanese and Spanish editions: Winter 2007)
IT Service Management based on ITIL V3 – A Pocket Guide (English and Dutch versions Autumn 2007, French, German, Japanese and Spanish editions: Winter 2007)
IT Service Management based on ITIL V3 – A Pocket Guide (English and Dutch versions Autumn 2007, French, German, Japanese and Spanish editions: Winter 2007)
Foundations of IT Service Management based on ITIL® (ITIL V2), (English, Dutch, French, German, Spanish, Japanese, Chinese, Danish, Italian, Korean, Russian, Arabic; also available as a CD-ROM)
Implementing Service and Support Management Processes (English)
IT Service Management - een samenvatting, 2de druk (Dutch)
Release and Control for IT Service Management, based on ITIL® - A Practitioner Guide (English)

ISO/IEC 20000

ISO/IEC 20000 - A Pocket Guide (English, Italian, German, Spanish, Portuguese)
ISO/IEC 20000 – An Introduction (English: Autumn 2007)
Implementing ISO/IEC 20000 (English: Autumn 2007)

ISO 27001 and ISO 17799

Information Security based on ISO 27001 and ISO 17799 - A Management Guide (English)
Implementing Information Security based on ISO 27001 and ISO 17799 - A Management Guide (English)

CobiT

IT Governance based on CobiT4® - A Management Guide (English, German)

IT Service CMM

IT Service CMM - A Pocket Guide (English)

ASL and BiSL

ASL - A Framework for Application Management (English)
ASL - Application Services Library - A Management Guide (English, Dutch)
BiSL - A Framework for Business Information Management (Dutch; English)
BiSL - Business information Services Library - A Management Guide (Dutch; English edition due Autumn 2007)

ISPL

IT Services Procurement op basis van ISPL (Dutch)
IT Services Procurement based on ISPL – A Pocket Guide (English)

IT Topics & Management instruments

De RfP voor IT-outsourcing (Dutch; English version due autumn 2007)
Decision- en Controlfactoren voor IT-Sourcing (Dutch)
Defining IT Success through the Service Catalog (English)
Frameworks for IT Management - An introduction (English, Japanese; German edition Autumn 2007)

Frameworks for IT Management – A Pocket Guide (Winter 2007)
Implementing leading standards for IT management (English, Dutch)
IT Service Management Best Practices, volumes 1, 2, 3 and 4 (Dutch)
ITSM from hell! / ITSM from hell based on Not ITIL (English)
ITSMP - The IT Strategy Management Process (English)
Metrics for IT Service Management (English)
Service Management Process Maps (English)
Six Sigma for IT Management (English)
Six Sigma for IT Management – A Pocket Guide (English)

MOF/MSF

MOF - Microsoft Operations Framework, A Pocket Guide (Dutch, English, French, German, Japanese)
MSF - Microsoft Solutions Framework, A Pocket Guide (English, German)

IT Architecture

TOGAF, The Open Group Architecture Framework – A Management Guide (English)
The Open Group Architecture Framework – 2007 Edition (English, official publication of TOG)
TOGAF™ Version 8 Enterprise Edition – Study Guide (English, official publication of TOG)

Quality Management

ISO 9000

ISO 9001:2000 - The Quality Management Process (English)

EFQM

The EFQM excellence model for Assessing Organizational Performance – A Management Guide (English)

Project/Programme/Risk Management

ICB

NCB – Nederlandse Competence Baseline (Dutch on behalf of IPMA-NL)
Handboek Projectmanagement voor IPMA-C en IPMA-D (Dutch, early 2008)

PRINCE2™

Project Management based on PRINCE2™- Edition 2005 (English, Dutch, German)
PRINCE2™ - A No Nonsense Management Guide (English)
PRINCE2™ voor opdrachtgevers – Management Guide (Dutch)

MINCE2®

MINCE2® – A Framework for Organizational Maturity (English)

MSP

Programme Management based on MSP (English, Dutch)
Programme Management based on MSP - A Management Guide (English)

M_o_R

Risk Management based on M_o_R - A Management Guide (English)

For the latest information on VHP publications, visit our website: www.vanharen.net

Service Management Strategies that Work: Guidance for Executives

Gary Case
Troy DuMoulin
George Spalding
Anil C. Dissanayake

Van Haren
PUBLISHING

Colophon

Title:	Service Management Strategies that Work: Guidance for Executives
Authors:	Gary Case
	Troy DuMoulin
	George Spalding
	Anil C. Dissanayake
Editor:	Jayne Wilkinson
Publisher:	Van Haren Publishing, Zaltbommel, NL
	www.vanharen.net
ISBN:	978 90 8753 048 8
Edition:	First edition, first impression, September 2007
Design and Layout:	CO2 Premedia, Amersfoort, NL
Printer:	Wilco, Amersfoort, NL

For further information about Van Haren Publishing, please send an email to info@vanharen.net

Contents

List of Figures and Tables

Figures

Tables

Acknowledgements

The Authors want to thank our fellow Pinkers for all of the support, passion and real world experience that we trust is reflected in these pages. As advisors and consultants we have the privilege of working with many strong and courageous organizations as they move forward in their IT Service Management journey. This collection of papers reflects some of our learning as we have assisted them in their transformation from technology to service organizations.

Pink Elephant would like to acknowledge the contributions of MCI.

About Pink Elephant

Pink Elephant is the world leader in IT management best practices, offering conferences, education, consulting services and ATLAS™ (a secure, web-enabled knowledge management system containing Pink's highly valued intellectual property), to public and private businesses globally. The company specializes in improving the quality of IT services through the application of recognized frameworks, including the IT Infrastructure Library (ITIL®). Pink Elephant has been involved in the 'ITIL project' since its inception in 1987, and was selected as an international expert to contribute to the ITIL V3 project. For more information, please visit www.pinkelephant.com.

Foreword

The Service Organization

It is the nature of ideas, processes, structures and functions to mature and change over time as the needs placed upon those concepts evolve. This is equally true of IT governance and the corresponding design of organizational structures and roles. The technology industry as a whole is undergoing a transformation, from one largely shaped by the leadership and personalities of individuals, to one that is becoming more defined, homogeneous and regulated. In parallel to this we see an evolution of IT management focus, moving away from a pure technology view to one focused on the needs and requirements of business partnership and integration.

To make the leap from technology management to business partnership, a cultural shift is required on the part of both the management staff of the IT organization, as well as the business customer they serve, to the effect that IT is recognized as an inherent and integral part of the business organization, as opposed to a unique and separate function.

It is precisely due to this understanding of interdependency that IT governance and legislation have established public reporting and audit requirements on IT processes and controls. The result of this awareness translates into the following statements:

- The financial results of a company are a direct result of its business processes.
- Business processes are dependent on, and automated by, IT services and systems.
- IT Services are directly impacted by the maturity and controls of IT processes.
- IT professionals have a direct impact on the consistency of IT processes.

From this perspective, the following are true:

- There is no separation between the business process and its underlying technology.
- IT organizations have to understand what services they provide, and implement the enterprise processes that deliver and support them.
- IT organizations have a business and legal requirement to understand and manage how IT services are built by technology components.
- IT governance and management structures have to be in place to manage both services and processes that span existing technology management silos.

This book represents a collection of advanced papers on various subjects related to the changing role of IT within a business focused service value network. Each paper was originally written as a discrete document and can stand alone on its content. The goal of this book is to assist organizations with understanding the impact of Service Management on various elements relating to IT Governance and to provide guidance on how to best apply a recommended approach.

Preface

IT Governance: A Compass without a Map?

Does your IT Governance output provide you with a detailed strategic blueprint and plan for business value generation, or is it a compass without a map?

Perhaps many of the IT management challenges that we face today are a reflection on the state of maturity of IT Governance structures and roles. This is due, in part, to the fact that many people disagree on the definition and role of IT Governance.

IT Governance is responsible for (defining, establishing and measuring) the enterprise IT (vision, strategy, policies, structures and capabilities) required to support business value generation and corporate governance requirements.

To use a building analogy, IT Governance is responsible for understanding business requirements, legislative constraints and technology opportunities. It then takes this knowledge and drafts the master blueprint and architecture for how to build, run and improve the IT organization.

In this blueprint key design decisions are documented:
• IT Accountability and decision-making framework
• Enterprise IT Policy
• The IT Service Portfolio and Architecture
• Organizational Structure and Supplier Model
• Operating Model, IT Capabilities/Processes
• Technology and IT Tool Standards
• IT Investment and Funding Models
• Performance Dashboard Characteristics

Based on this blueprint, it is the responsibility of IT Management (the skilled tradesmen who build based on the blueprint) to adopt, implement and comply with the established vision and strategies; however, it remains the responsibility of IT Governance to ensure that management does in fact implement and remains in compliance with the established blueprint. Without these elements clearly documented and communicated, IT management and project investment decisions are made blindly in isolation without consideration of, or in alignment with, an enterprise IT strategy.

The key words from this summary are **define**, **establish** and **measure**. The responsibility of IT Governance includes, but extends beyond, setting high level principles, policy and decision-making models (the compass). Unless IT Governance defines the details around its operating model (the map), the vision and strategy is limited and without context or direction.

The central problem is that many organizations view the role of IT Governance as too heavenly minded to be much earthly good. Their approach goes as far as developing a high level vision and strategy, but falls short of defining enough detail to support the creation of the IT organization they envision. Or, at the very least, what is defined at an executive level is not effectively communicated down to an operational level.

However, defining vision/strategy and establishing a blueprint is still only two out of the three key activities. To be ultimately successful, an executive-level measurement model or dashboard needs to be established for all aspects of the blueprint. The purpose of this dashboard is to initially create a baseline in order to identify gaps and priorities, and then to support continual improvement and ensure organizational compliance – what is not measured is not done!

This book will provide insight and strategies that work and are intended to support the creation of this blueprint.

1

Introduction

Business Alignment or Business Integration?

Many books and papers have been written on the subject of IT and business alignment. While not to downplay this important topic, one needs to ask why we are having this conversation. You don't see the equivalent concerns about HR and business alignment, Finance and business alignment or Engineering and business alignment. The very fact that these are relevant topics today tells us something about the current level of maturity of our industry.

Most IT organizations around the world are at the very early stages of a technology to service evolution. The challenge before us is to convince both the IT 'Techie' and the business customer that IT does not simply manage hardware and software.

As IT organizations evolve into a Service Delivery model, it is important to understand where the industry has come from and how Technology Management differs in focus from Service Management. Over the last 20 years IT planning, strategy, recruitment, skills training and incentive programs have focused on developing centers of technology excellence. We have hired and trained individuals to hone their technology skills in order to optimize and reduce cost around the use of new technology innovations. However, for the most part, education around a business perspective has largely been ignored. Nowhere is this clearer than the fact that, until very recently, most computer science degrees have been purely technology-focused and have little or no focus on teaching general business acumen.

There is a growing awareness that there is no real separation between the business process and the technology that underpins it. How do you separate Accounts Payable from SAP? Or, from a different perspective, why is the engineering group that builds an oil platform and the IT department that works along side them, to hook it up to the information network, seen as having a different position in the business organization. One group is considered as a business unit and the other as something unique and separate. The answer, of course, has to be that they are both enabling business functions and are not really different at all.

Perhaps the only real difference is a matter of time and the awareness of dependency and complete integration.

1.1 Organizing IT – The Traditional Manufacturing Model

Since the early industrial revolution and the advent of modern manufacturing processes, pioneered by men such as Henry Ford for his famous Model T automobile, organizational design has focused on breaking apart complex processes into the smallest individual tasks.

The primary reasons for this decision were that, at the turn of the last century, the general workforce lacked highly skilled resources, since the majority of employees had recently moved from a rural cottage industry to an urban industrial model. In addition to the skills shortage, early industry was faced with severe challenges regarding general communication and collaboration tools. This created a need to simplify each person's task down to a set of focused and repeated activities.

However, as the organization still required the ability to maintain a fuller picture of the entire process, it created a foreman or manager position, to oversee a small set of related tasks performed by individuals, and then a middle manager to supervise that foreman and his related peers. Following on from this model, a senior manager was needed to oversee a set of middle managers who, in turn, managed similar teams. The resulting organization was comprised of large vertically oriented management pyramids or silos, focused on groups of like activities, where communication was relatively efficient vertically through the pyramid, but was extremely challenged when collaboration was required between silos. This management structure of task segmentation, coupled with the need to create layers of management roles to hold the bigger picture together, was the only practical way to accomplish large and complex objectives within the limitations facing the early industrial age. Thus was born our modern day organizational design.

To summarize: The only way for large groups of individuals to collaborate in complex processes, such as building a car, was to give each of them only one thing to do, and let them focus on doing that one thing to the mental exclusion of everything else.
For example, your job is to put brake pedals on the cars as they move past; you will do this as efficiently and as quickly as possible; this is what you are paid to do, nothing else; anything you do outside this task is someone else's job. These management structures are still used today, even though many of the reasons for their creation no longer apply.

In an IT context, this translates into management silos that are created around like technology domains or platforms, such as servers, databases or applications. Today in IT, you can see the culture of task segmentation clearly when the individuals in these entrenched silos, such as network administrators or application developers, believe fervently that they are doing the Service Desk a favor if they fix something. In their minds, responding to incidents is someone else's job. The inherent problem with task segmentation is that, by the very act of breaking down the complex processes into individual tasks or activities, those who perform the individual tasks do not always understand the overall picture. For example, an IT service such as e-mail is never found within a single technology domain but is comprised of applications, servers, databases, etc. When we fail to understand clearly how an IT service is built, we lose critical management information.

We have lost sight of the forest by focusing on the trees.

Or perhaps an even more accurate statement is that we don't have a forest or trees problem, we have a bark problem – we are far too close to the technology issues to even envision that we have a problem.

To extend the car analogy just a bit further, compare the current management of IT based on technology silos to a *hypothetical* automobile repair shop that hires and focuses primarily on highly specialized mechanics, as opposed to also recruiting and training general practitioners. In this scenario they have recruited and hired the best wheel mechanics in the market. No one can remove tires faster or more efficiently than their technicians. They have developed entire certification models and career paths focused on this one activity. They base their performance evaluations entirely on how well they perform this specific activity and they get what they measure. However, these same star individuals would think nothing of whipping the tire off the car when it's moving down the highway rather than waiting until it is parked safely in the driveway (this may sound unlikely, but is exactly what happens when IT makes a change without consideration of the greater business impact). From their perspective, if they see any indication that the tire needs replacing, they do it immediately and efficiently without consideration that the car is an integrated solution. This is in effect how we manage and operate IT in a technology-focused IT organization which is not focused on, or aware of the business processes they support.

In this model the specialists know that there is a car, but it is the conceptual element that they do not comprehend. They certainly do not understand the full implication of the wheel (server, switch, application) to the car. They are probably aware of the axle, but little else. It would not occur to them to ask the driver whether now was a good time to change the tire, since they have never met him. In short, in this analogy the repair shop (IT) has specialized by task segmentation to the point where the staff have lost sight of the purpose of the task.

Similar to the automobile repair shop analogy, IT needs general mechanics as well as specialists that understand the entire workings and relationship of the major systems to support the service, in this example called *driver transportation*. IT performance measures currently focus on domain and technology management. Organizations that define horizontal IT services will also require performance measures related to the governance of services and processes.

The concept of general practitioner and specialist can also be observed in the medical profession, where there are general practitioners who understand the needs of holistic patient care as well as specialists who have expert knowledge in specific areas. However, historically and due to the incentive programs we have deployed, IT has a disproportionate number of highly specialized technicians in relation to general mechanics.

> *"Effective managers have long known that you manage by processes ... what's new is the enabling technology ... the less developed information systems that supported command-and-control structures couldn't do that. In fact, those structures – which can probably be traced back to the church and to the military as far back as Caesar – persisted precisely because for many years they were the only way to manage large complex organizations."*

Source: P. Allaire Chairman and Chief Executive Officer, Director of Xerox

■ 1.2 Technology vs Service Management

The evolution of a Service Management perspective begins with an awareness that a rudimentary responsibility of IT is to understand what services it provides. Following this, the second question then becomes: *How does any given IT component support an IT service which enables key business processes?* Until these two questions are understood, it is difficult to claim that IT is aligned with business goals. How do you claim to be aligned or integrated with the business if you don't understand what IT services are, how they are built and how they are consumed by a business customer to produce products or generate revenue?

Have you ever stopped to consider that ITIL® is a Service Management Framework?

It sounds pretty basic and you may be wondering what is meant by this obvious statement. Consider that if ITIL is a Service Management framework this means that all of the processes have only one goal: To plan for, deliver and support IT services.

■ 1.3 Linear Service Catalogs vs. Dynamic Service Portfolios

While ITIL has always been referred to as an IT Service Management Framework, the primary focus up until now has been on the 10 Service Support and Delivery processes. In previous versions of ITIL, the concept of a 'service' has almost been an afterthought, or at least something you would get to later. Consider that in ITIL v2 the process of Service Level Management has, as one of its many deliverables, a Service Catalog, which can be summarized from the theory as a brochure of IT Services where IT publishes the services it provides with their default characteristics and attributes or Linear Service Catalog.

In contrast to this, a Dynamic Service Portfolio can be interpreted as the product of a strategic process where service strategy and design conceive of and create services that are built and transitioned into the production environment based on business value. From this point, an actionable service catalog represents the published services, and is the starting point or basis for service operations and ongoing business engagement. The services documented in this catalog are bundled together into 'fit-for-purpose' offerings which are then subscribed to as a collection and consumed by business units.

But what happens if an IT organization does not have services defined? Well then perhaps ITIL in its full application has limited value at this point in an organization's maturity.

This is one of the primary reasons it continues to be a challenge to sell the benefits of IT Service Management to some companies. If the IT executive understands its total job to be the management and optimization of technology domains, and has little or no understanding or concern for what IT Services are, then the ITIL processes have limited value.

However, if it is understood that no technology component exists simply for its own right and that the individual components from various domains actually work together in connected cross platform systems that support IT services, then there is a significant need for enterprise IT processes that ensure a consistent delivery and support of those services.

In order to further understand the design of an IT organization that is based on services, it is important to define an IT service.

1.3.1 IT Service:

One or more technical or professional IT capabilities which enable a business process. Or from an ITIL version 3 perspective: 'A service is a means of delivering value to customers by facilitating outcomes customers want to achieve without the ownership of specific costs and risks.'

An IT service exhibits the following characteristics:

- fulfills one or more needs of the customer
- supports the customer's business objectives
- is perceived by the customer as a coherent whole or consumable product

Note: By this definition a service is a capability, not a technology solution or vertical domain such as a server environment or a business application.

Perhaps the easiest way to understand what a service is, is to consider the Application Service Provider (ASP model). In this model a business unit contracts for the capability of Client Relationship Management (CRM). The ASP manages all of the technical aspects of delivering this application service with the business customer only caring about the outcome of being able to enable and automate their CRM processes.

1.3.2 IT System:

An integrated composite that consists of one or more of the processes, hardware, software, facilities and people, that provides a capability to satisfy a stated need or objective.

An IT system:

- is a collection of resources and configuration items or assets that are necessary to deliver an IT Service
- is sometimes referred to as a Technology Solution

Note: The technology system is the complete composite of IT components from various domains which, when brought together in a relationship, represent a value-added technology solution: for example, a Local Area Network or an application system such as an Enterprise Resource Planning solution. A system is not referring to the application as a stand-alone element, but to all of the components which build the complete solution (application, databases, servers and middleware, etc.).

1.3.3 Configuration Item (CI):

- CIs are a component of an IT infrastructure that is part of an IT system.

- CIs may vary widely in complexity size and type – from a document or policy to an entire system or a single module or a minor hardware component.

■ 1.4 Technical and Professional Services:

When defining IT Services it is necessary to understand that there are two basic types of services that IT provide. These two types can be loosely classified as either 'Technical' or 'Professional' services.

A 'Technical Service' is defined as a technology-based capability that the customer consumes or uses in order to facilitate a business process or function. Or a component service which supports another IT Service which is customer facing. Technical services can be further understood as either application services or infrastructure services.

1.4.1 Examples of Technical Services

General infrastructure services such as:

- messaging/email
- file/print
- network or internet access
- office or desktop productivity
- voice communications
- application hosting
- storage management

Application-based services such as:

- financial management systems
- HR support
- power generation applications
- refining and control systems

Note: It is best practice to name the application-based service as closely as possible to the name of the business process it supports. This will be a critical step in understanding the business impact of IT service or component failure.

When the IT service names are aligned with business processes, both the business customer and IT staff have a clearer understanding of how technology is aligned to meet business objectives.

A 'Professional Service' is defined as the value-added activities that IT staff provide in order to support, maintain, monitor or ensure the consistent and reliable delivery of the technical services.

1.4.2 Examples of Professional Services

- IT architecture and engineering
- IT security
- IT support
- project management services
- IT consulting
- application development and enhancement services

Note: It is very important that the IT organization takes the time to define professional services, since in most organizations over 60% of the annual IT budget is spent on these activities. If these services are not defined, all of this cost is reported as a non-value-added overhead. In summary, the organization that does not define as many valued-added professional services as possible looks very 'fat' when IT management is considering outsourcing.

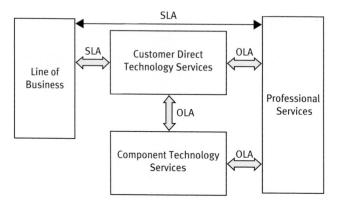

Figure 1.1: Service Dependency Model

In alignment with ITIL best practices, Service Level Agreements (SLAs) are developed between the business customer and IT, for those services which are customer facing. Internal Operational Level Agreements (OLAs) are developed for those services which support the delivery of customer direct services.

For example:

There is a customer facing SLA for the application service called Investment Banking, and it is supported by the following OLAs from component and professional services:

• application hosting
• storage
• data / LAN
• security management
• IT service continuity

There is a customer facing SLA for the infrastructure service called Desktop Automation which is supported by the following OLAs from supporting component and professional services:

• file / print
• incident management
• backup and recovery
• image management

To summarize, when a technology-focused IT organization does not understand IT services, it is challenging to create a strong enough business case for deploying ITIL processes and best practices. It is likely they will see some value in the support processes such as Incident, Problem and Change Management. However, it is likely that they will go no further until the concept of an IT service is understood and appreciated. Why would a company ever do true Configuration Management, full Release Management or Service Level Management unless it needed to know how the technology comes together to deliver end-to-end services modeled in the CMDB?

An organization's readiness to address full Service Management and the resulting need to address the IT organizational structures related to it can be tracked through an observable cultural maturity model.

1.4.3 Level 1 – IT is project and portfolio focused but operationally challenged

Good processes and controls exist to evaluate, control and execute projects in order to ensure on time, on scope and on budget delivery of initiatives. However, once those projects arrive in production, the controls evaporate. In this model, little to no concern is given to the processes which need to receive and support the project deliverables once they are live. For this organization, Service Management disciplines makes sense while the project is being developed, but are not a concern once the project is closed, since the attention of management is now focused on the next big initiative. Alternatively to the controls and processes evaporating, it is also possible to see each project defining and deploying its own support processes for each major project. This results in many redundant and unconnected processes and tools since they are project specific.

1.4.4 Level 2 – IT realizes that availability and reliability of technology is tied to business success

At this point IT governance focus is shared between project execution and the management and optimization of an IT technology environment. Domain or IT platform owners are established, and multiple business cases are developed and approved to purchase domain focused monitoring tools. Each domain acquires its own technology to monitor its own assets from a variety of different vendors. If configuration information is managed regarding the technology components, it is typically represented by inventory lists maintained by each functional group to the level of integrity required by that group. At this point of maturity, the organization has begun to implement basic support functions such as Service Desk and Change Management but is struggling with compliance.

1.4.5 Level 3 – IT acknowledges that technology components do not live in mythical isolation

When an IT organization realizes that availability and reliability have to be looked at from an end-to-end solution or, in ITIL words, a service view, the need for a service orientation and for the CMDB become an issue. It is also at this point that the organization is ready to support the development and implementation of the processes that are required to keep a central source of data up-to-date.

■ 1.5 The New Service Orientation – Organizational Model

Without a service perspective as described in the previous section, the IT organization focuses primarily on the management of technology domains as large stand alone silos. While it is important to manage these silos well in respect to domain-based goals related to availability, capacity, security and financial accountability, these goals represent only a basic level of IT management accountability.

The two largest of the traditional silos found within an IT organization are those involved in the separation of the application groups from the infrastructure management organization (Figure 1.2). Within each of these two major silos, there are additional management structures based on application types or technology platforms. On the positive side of this model, each group manages its domain or platform budget and objectives with reasonable effectiveness; however, little to no thought is given to enterprise IT planning and Service Delivery except by the most senior of IT management staff. On the negative side of this model, we see frequent attempts to define SLAs based on the application in isolation of its supporting system components. Or conversely, we see a customer-facing SLA presented, based on a group of back office technology components, such as servers which are never consumed directly.

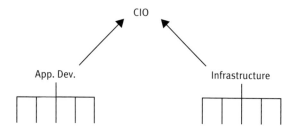

Figure 1.2: Traditional IT Silos

Another very common business engagement model found in a technology focused organization is represented in Figure 1.3. This diagram presents a picture where the primary business or client relationship is owned by the application organization. In this model, the infrastructure group is often perceived to be a service provider to the application organization. This is made even more complex when the application development groups are perceived to be part of business units and are not managed or considered to be part of the enterprise IT organization.

Note: This picture represents a typical IT relationship model. ITIL terminology refers to the agreement between the application and infrastructure groups as an operational level agreement as opposed to an SLA.

Service levels are typically developed between the Application Development organization and the business client, and supporting agreements are established between the Application

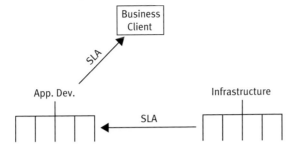

Figure 1.3: Business Engagement Model - Application Development ownership of client relationships

and Infrastructure Organizations. While this seems reasonable on the surface, it promotes several long-term negative management results.

1. It promotes a belief that the application is somehow superior, separate and distinct from the other supporting components that make up the service.
2. It promotes a belief that the application groups have a more important place in a Service Delivery model.
3. It promotes a belief that the application group is a client of the infrastructure group as opposed to a partner for delivering end-to-end IT services to the true customer which is the business.

In this traditional model, application groups gain the upper hand in business – IT discussions and the infrastructure organization are relegated to perceived second class or largely unimportant functions.

The end result of this model often plays out in the following scenario:

Each year, the IT budgeting process allocates funding to only a set number of IT projects based on available resources. Since the application groups have the direct relationship to the business customer, they typically receive the lion's share of available money for their projects. This leaves many of the proposed infrastructure maintenance and upgrade projects without funding. This scenario plays out year after year, with the inevitable consequence of the infrastructure becoming outdated and unstable. The end result of this model is that the overall service, which is never the application in isolation, is placed in jeopardy and begins to degrade.

The application of a best practice Project Portfolio Management practice is designed to avoid this scenario (Figure 1.4). In principle, Portfolio Management is an enterprise process which considers, prioritizes and approves all requests for new projects in relationship to business strategy and objectives. However, for this principle to work according to the intent, it requires the Project Management Office (PMO) to be an enterprise governance function and process that takes an unbiased view of all project requests.

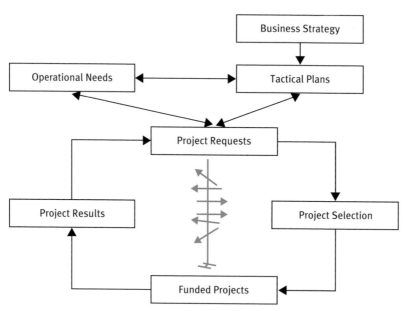

Figure 1.4: Portfolio Management

However, in many organizations the Project Management processes are managed within silos or at best, at an Application vs. Infrastructure Management level. So, the end result is that project prioritization is not done at an enterprise level and the earlier scenario is all too real for many IT organizations.

This discussion about Portfolio Management and the concepts of enterprise IT services points to a required change in approach of IT organizational design to incorporate governance and ownership models that support the management of functions that have objectives, services and processes spanning the traditional technology silos depicted in Figure 1.2.

■ 1.6 Service Oriented IT Organizational Models

IT services, as well as the ITIL processes that support them, inevitably span multiple organizational structures. In essence, IT services and their supporting processes can be understood as horizontal management structures which are established and managed on top of the traditional vertical silos. As these services and processes are defined, a need becomes apparent to establish governance and ownership roles that do not seem to fit well in the traditional vertical silos.

1.6.1   The Impact of Classic Job Descriptions on a Service Organization

Based on the historical context of task segmentation, the average person has a unique set of tasks and activities defined within their job description related to their specific silo. However, there have always been three types of work they perform on a daily basis, but only one type of work is typically documented in their formal HR job description (Figure 1.5). We might refer to the specific set of tasks within their silo as their functional work.

Examples: a network administrator, an application programmer, a service desk agent, an IT security manager. In each of these examples, the individual has a job function within a traditional IT silo where they spend a certain portion of their day. However, each of these individuals can also be assigned to temporary project work. What is equally true is that each individual will spend a certain portion of their time involved in cross-functional processes which they will deem as time spent helping someone else's job (eg they have always been involved in fixing things that break, going to meetings about things that are changing, or moving things around based on requests). In other words, they have always been involved in Service Management processes, but because these activities are not formally defined as part of their job function, they regard time spent in those activities as time spent away from their real jobs.

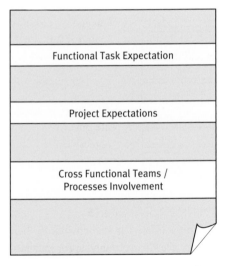

Figure 1.5: Job Description – types of work

The reality is that each individual has always been involved in three types of work long before ITIL or Service Management came along. What is new is that what was before undefined and unmeasured is now being formalized. From an individual perspective, moving to a Service Management model eventually requires the opening of job description documentation in order to adjust expectations and performance measures around work which is conducted on all three types of work.

Several organizations that have made project management improvements have recently included the definition of project related expectations in their IT employee job descriptions, but even those companies which are tracking resource time against both functional and project-related work still neglect to track time spent in cross-functional process work. In essence, what is not defined cannot be managed. Perhaps one of the reasons that many of us find ourselves always with too little time to get all that we need done in a given day and end up responding to email at 10:00 pm is that we only account for one or at most two types of the work that we are involved in.

1.6.2 Horizontal Management Structures Create a Management Matrix

What occurs when an organization defines enterprise IT services and process is that two new virtual horizontal organizational structures are established on top of the traditional vertical IT domain-based silos (Figure 1.6). The end result of this decision is the establishment of a matrix organization where individuals within IT have multiple lines of accountability.

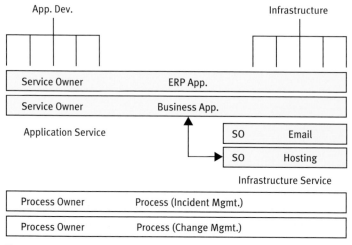

Figure 1.6: Matrix IT Organization

For example, an individual who is a database administrator (DBA) is responsible to their functional manager for domain based duties; however, they are also responsible for database components that are used for multiple IT services and have to work with multiple service owners. By the nature of those databases being part of multiple IT services, they also participate in the ITSM processes described by ITIL, and are consistently asked to participate in process-related tasks and meetings. On top of this is the need to work on project related work with the consistent nagging of a project manager, and the poor DBA has at least four different roles pressuring them for resource and time prioritization.

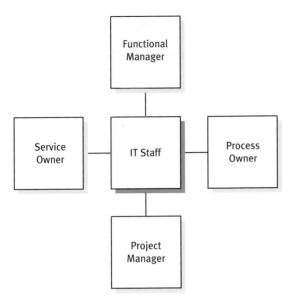

Figure 1.7: Matrix Roles

Matrix Roles:

1. Functional Manager
2. Service Owner
3. Process Owner
4. Project Manager

With the implementation of Service Management, the concept of matrix accountability is unavoidable. A critical success factor in dealing with the resulting matrix is having a clear understanding of the new roles, and establishing clear policies and guidelines to understand how an individual IT resource prioritizes their time against all four areas.

For the purposes of this document, it is assumed that the role of a functional and project manager is well understood. The two new roles that Service Management introduces to the mix are the roles of Service Owner and Process Owner (Figure 1.7).

■ 1.7 The Service Owner Role

The Service Owner is accountable for a specific service within an organization regardless of where the technology components or professional capabilities reside which build it. Service ownership is as critical to Service Management as establishing ownership for processes which cross multiple silos or departments.

To ensure that a service is managed with a business focus, the definition of a single point of accountability is absolutely essential to provide the level of attention and focus required for its delivery.

Much like a Process Owner, the Service Owner is responsible for continuous improvement and the management of change affecting the services under their care. The Service Owner is a primary stakeholder in all of the IT processes which enable or support the service they own. For example:

- **Incident Management:** involved in or perhaps chairs the crisis management team for high-priority incidents impacting the service owned
- **Problem Management:** plays a major role in establishing the root cause and proposed permanent fix for the service being evaluated
- **Release Management:** is a key stakeholder in determining whether a new release affecting a service in production is ready
- **Change Management:** participates in Change Advisory Board decisions, approving changes to the services they own
- **Configuration Management:** ensures that all groups which maintain the data and relationships for the service architecture they are responsible for have done so with the level of integrity required
- **Service Level Management:** acts as the single point of contact for a specific service and ensures that the Service Catalog is accurate in relationship to their service
- **Availability and Capacity Management:** reviews technical data from a domain perspective to ensure that the needs of the overall service are being met
- **IT Service Continuity Management:** understands and is responsible for ensuring that all elements required to restore their service are known and in place in the event of a crisis
- **IT Financial Management:** assists in defining and tracking the cost models in relationship to how their service is costed and recovered

■ 1.8 The Process Owner Role

The initial planning phase of any ITIL project must include establishing the role of Process Owner. This key role is accountable for the overall quality of the process and oversees the management of, and organizational compliance to the process flows, procedures, data models, policies, and technologies associated with the IT business process.

The Process Owner performs the essential role of Process Champion, Design Lead, Advocate, Coach and Protector. Typically, a Process Owner should be a senior level manager with credibility, influence and authority across the various areas impacted by the activities of the process. The Process Owner is required to have the ability to influence and ensure compliance to the policies and procedures put in place across the cultural and departmental silos of the IT organization.

A Process Owner's job is not necessarily to do the hands-on process re-engineering and process improvement, but to ensure that it gets done. He or she typically assembles the project team, obtains the resources that the team requires, protects the team from internal politics, and works to gain co-operation of the other executives and managers whose functional groups are involved in the process. This role's responsibilities do not end with the successful embedding of a new process. In a process-oriented organization, the Process Owner remains responsible for the integrity, communication, functionality, performance, compliance and business relevance of the process.

The three major activities of the Process Owner are Process Design, Organizational Awareness, and Advocacy.

1.8.1 Process Design

- Accountable for the ongoing business value and integrity of the process design across the functional and organizational boundaries the process crosses:

  - process and procedures
  - policies
  - process roles
  - Key Performance Indicators (KPIs)
  - process automation requirements
  - process integrations

1.8.2 Organizational Awareness

- Accountable for planning and implementing practices, orientation and training to ensure organizational understanding and adoption of the process activities:

  - internal and external training
  - new employee on-boarding and orientation
  - one-on-one mentoring
  - teambuilding exercises
  - conflict facilitation
  - communication and feedback forums

1.8.3 Advocacy

- Accountable for protecting, measuring and reporting on process compliance across organizational silos:

  - dealing with political issues in relationship to process compliance
  - promoting a culture of process collaboration
  - breaking down strong silo or functional mindsets

- verifying process compliance on an ongoing basis
- representing IT processes to business
- managing process exceptions
- promoting integration with other processes

While design and organizational learning can be delegated to other process roles, it is not advisable to ever delegate advocacy.

With the definitions of Service and Process Owner within the IT organizational structure, the burning question then becomes: 'where do we establish these new service and process roles?'

In both cases, these horizontal roles represented are as effective or not according to the level of empowerment given to the role by the executives of the IT organization.

Caution: *Frequently, Service or Process Ownership roles are established with no real authority or direct escalation path for issues of non compliance and continuous improvement.*

The answer to this question is that there are two primary models for placing ownership:

1. establish horizontal ownership within an existing vertical structure
2. establish horizontal ownership outside the traditional silos in a new vertical silo focused on the management of enterprise IT objectives

Neither model is inherently right or wrong, but will be applied as logic dictates. However, our experience is that the second model presented in this document has a greater likelihood of long-term success.

■ 1.9 Placing Ownership Within Existing Structures

The first model places Service and Process Ownership within the existing vertical organization structures (Figure 1.8). The general premise of this option is that no major changes are made to the existing silos and that ownership is established within an existing group that has a sympathetic or vested interest in the service or process. It is very common for an organization which is just starting to adopt Service Management to apply this model at an early stage of their initiatives. However, while this provides an easier transition with minimal disruption to the existing organization in the first stages of Service Management, many organizations will adopt the second approach described in this document over time.

Examples:

- ownership of Incident Management is given to the Service Desk
- ownership of Release Management is given to the group responsible for production assurance
- ownership of the email Service is given to the group which administers the primary application
- ownership of the Voice service is placed with the Telecommunications group

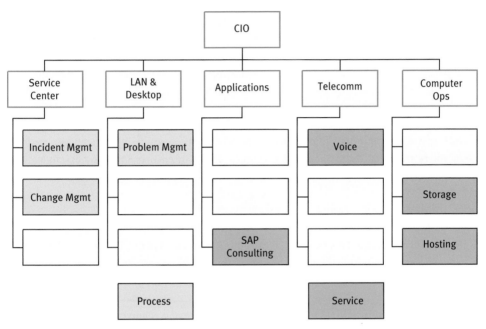

Figure 1.8: Ownership Model 1: Placing ownership within existing structures

This model offers both pros and cons when adopted:

Pros:

- This approach does not require major organizational changes, in that ownership is established within the existing structure and typically existing resources.
- Advocacy and decision-making related to the process or service works well within the silo in which the ownership is placed.
- Service ownership works well in this model since there is typically a primary point of contact established for the IT service within the existing structure.

Cons:

- An important message that Service Management attempts to establish is that services and processes are agnostic to organizational structure and that they are delivered through the co-operation of multiple IT groups or domains working together to deliver IT services. By establishing the ownership within an existing structure this model inevitable works against this goal by sending a subtle message that the Process Ownership belongs to a certain department or group.
- Whether the organization implementing the services and processes realizes it or not, a matrix organization is being created. In this model, the matrix is not immediately visible since no changes have been made to the existing structures. However, the moment a Change Manager role is established, an IT resource now has responsibilities to both their functional manager as well as to the Process Owner. This matrix accountability is not as apparent in this model. There are decision-making limitations inherent in this approach as well, as accountability issues can surface from the frequently encountered comment, 'you can't tell me what to do'.
- In this model, it is common to give Process Ownership to someone who already has a full time role within the functional group in which they reside. This leads to conflicts of interest in relation to time and resources which often place the process focus at a disadvantage.

1.9.1 Implementation Approach:

- **Service Ownership:** This model makes sense for Service Ownership, since even though few IT services exist exclusively within only one IT group, there is still a primary organization which provides the management interface for the service, eg Hosting – Computer Ops; Virus Management – IT Security.
- **Process Ownership:** This approach is often employed and is relatively effective in the early stages of a process implementation project. However, over time it is difficult to maintain this model since, unlike IT Services, the processes have no affinity to one specific group. Couple this with the people resource and bandwidth issues that inevitably occur, and it is usually understood that Process Ownership is better established outside the traditional organizational structures. While this is true for the central process governance roles, the more day-to-day operational roles are typically still distributed across the various groups of the organization.

Note: Establishing Process Ownership within existing structures works reasonably well for a smaller organization or one that has implemented a limited number of processes. However, once the scope of process governance is required to span multiple IT organizations or business units, this model begins to break down and a separate function focused on Service Delivery is required, as is explained in the next section.

1.10 A New Organizational Construct – The IT Service Delivery Function

The alterative approach to placing Service and Process Ownership within existing structures and departments is to create a new structure within IT reporting directly to the CIO (Figure 1.9). Many organizations designate this new organizational group as the Service Delivery or Service Management function. The function is typically led by a senior IT executive who manages a set of roles responsible for the governance and ownership of Service Management processes that span the entire IT function.

While this description represents the ideal placement for this function, many organizations introduce the ITSM processes through an infrastructure initiative and may not have the ability to establish an organization structure which has an enterprise IT governance mandate. For this scenario, it is not uncommon to see the new Service Delivery function report to the head of the infrastructure organization. While this is not ideal, it can be the first step in applying this model.

Depending on the size of the organization or the transactional volume of the processes, a small team of individuals may support these central process roles. However, these roles are primarily involved in process governance, reporting and continuous improvement. The majority of the process activities are typically still performed by individuals distributed within the other organizational structures and groups.

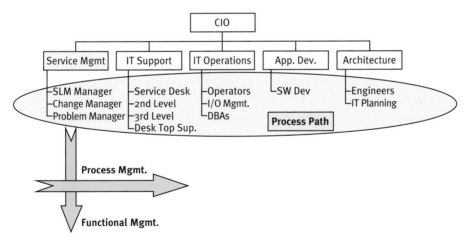

Figure 1.9: Ownership Model 2: IT Service Delivery function

Pros:

- This model sends a clear message to the IT organization that processes cross the entire IT function. Unlike the previous model, this approach creates an explicit matrix and emphasizes the fact that that Process Ownership is outside a traditional IT domain or technology platform. The existence of a matrix is unavoidable in both models; however, the best way to deal with a matrix is to clearly acknowledge that you have one and then develop clear policies and guidelines to help individuals know how and when to prioritize their time.
- The new organizational structure and roles sends a clear message to the IT groups and domains that Senior Management supports the implementation and governance of management processes.
- This organizational structure is especially beneficial to global (multi-national) companies who expect consistent operations, but must attend to local staffing and operational needs.
- This model removes any potential conflict of interest when an individual reports to a functional manager and represents the interests of an enterprise process.
- By establishing Process Ownership with a single individual outside of the existing organizational structure, the designated Process Owner can typically handle more than one process, unless the size of the organization makes this difficult.

Cons:

- While it is very common to have a single individual who owns more that one process, this model typically requires the creation of new resource requirements and the implementation of a significant organizational change. However, the additional staffing required should result in a limited impact to the organization. The efficiencies of the model and productivity improvements in the functional groups will satisfy the increased staffing required to support the matrix group.
- This organizational structure can be stigmatized as a staff function, as it seems to be more governance in nature than operational. Attention must be given to ensure that clear deliverables and responsibilities are established in the group's charter.

1.10.1 Implementation Approach:

- **Service Ownership:** For Service Ownership this model makes sense only when the organization is large enough to have multiple regions offering the same service. In this instance, the global or regional service governance and ownership can be overseen by a central role focused on overall service planning and co-ordination, while Service Delivery is maintained locally.
- **Process Ownership:** This model is the recommended approach for establishing centralized Process Ownership within a vertically organized IT organization. As indicated earlier, it is the process governance, ownership and measurement that is centralized – not the operational task execution.

■ 1.11 Service Level Management and the Service Organization

As discussed in the previous section, IT services are supported and delivered by IT processes. However, both of these elements are delivered and managed as horizontal elements within a traditional vertical structure organized around technology domains.

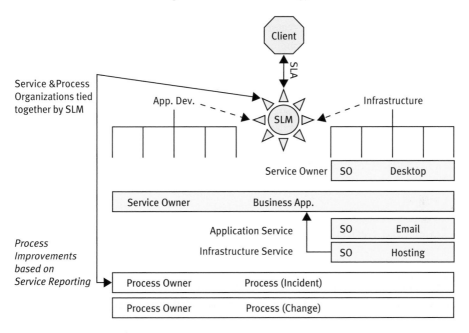

Figure 1.10: SLM as the face of IT to the customer

In this environment, the Service Level Management (SLM) process plays a critical role. The SLM process and roles provide a single face of IT to the business customer (Figure 1.10). SLM also ties together the traditional silo-based organization, while providing guidance and policy around resource prioritization based on established Service Delivery agreements.

In this model, the relationship of IT as an enterprise service organization is front-ended by the SLM process. It is supported by the establishment of a Service Catalog from which the roles of SLM engage with and negotiate SLAs.

The key element of this model is that IT is presented as a single provider to the business customer. This remains true regardless of whether or not elements of the IT services are outsourced to external providers. SLM and its Service Catalog provide a single face for IT to the business from which it can define the delivery of end-to-end services.

SLM, by its definition of IT services in the Service Catalog, provides the critical business context and prioritization required by IT to ensure that its actions reflect the best interests of the stated goals of the business. The gathering of requirements and the establishment of business-facing service agreements drive the development and improvement of the processes which support them.

The SLM process has as its focus:

1. the establishment of business requirements
2. the identification of new services required by the business
3. the measurement of Service Delivery against these requirements
4. the reporting of how these services are being delivered to the business partner
5. the identification of where improvements need to be made within IT services and or the processes which deliver them

In essence, SLM plays an important role in a Service Management focused organization in that it facilitates the definition and management of IT services. The SLM process provides guidelines for collaboration with the management roles of Technology Domains, Services and Processes.

 ## 1.12 The Evolution of the Service Delivery Organization

A key focus of ITIL V3 is the design and management of the service portfolio within the context of a Value Service Network. The central premise of the Value Service Network is that there are three primary types of IT service providers that work together in an integrated model to provide value based service outcomes to business customers.

The three primary provider types discussed in this Value Network are:

1. IT service providers which are embedded within and are funded by a specific business unit in order to focus on the needs of that customer
2. external IT service providers which provide contracted services either to an internal IT service provider or directly to the business customer
3. shared service providers which provide common IT services to all business units at varying levels based on need

A critical aspect of IT strategy is defining the right mix of all three types and then ensuring that common processes and tools are deployed across the entire Value Service Network in order to ensure that each service provider delivers their services collectively, in accordance with business requirements and agreements.

An interesting trend, that can be observed in many IT organizations today, is the evolution of a shared services group that focuses on aspects of Enterprise IT Governance and Service Delivery. One of the primary drivers behind its gradual creation, is the challenge of managing a complex Value Service Network without a central governance function, which exists and

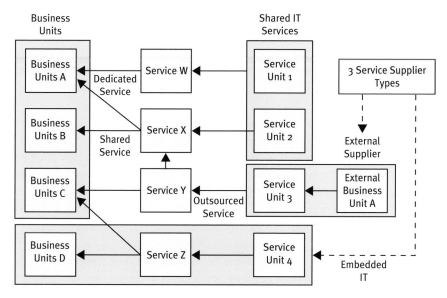

Figure 1.11 – Value Service Network

is empowered to work at a level spanning all of the various IT silos, managed by the three provider types.

In many companies today the historical context of task segmentation discussed earlier in this book has largely left the governance of IT in a distributed state. The result of this distribution is that groups, that by right should have an enterprise mandate and authority, find themselves located in an infrastructure or application based silo, with a conflict of interest on one hand and a lack of authority outside of their particular silo on the other. As IT organizations realize this challenge, they begin to extract out of the traditional IT infrastructure and application silos the groups and functions that provide a shared enterprise governance service.

The concept of a shared services organization is not new to IT. For reasons of efficiency and lower transactional costs, IT organizations have been consolidating shared infrastructure, networks, data centers and major business applications for several years. However, a more recent trend is the consolidation of professional service groups into a new shared services organization, focused not only on technology optimization and cost reduction, but on ensuring the delivery of business value from strategic IT services.

As organizations become aware that services are agnostic to technology silos, they also understand that many of the professional services they provide, such as project management, consulting, internal audit, application development, IT Service Management, engineering and architecture, need to be standardized, integrated and centralized for reasons of both efficiency as well as governance oversight. The centralization of these groups and their eventual consolidation under a single shared services model is what this book refers to as the 'Evolving Service Delivery Organization.'

For example, many organizations have already established a separate corporate Project Management Office (PMO), or have created an IT Security and Risk Management group as separate IT functions that now reside outside the traditional application and infrastructure silos. Some IT organizations have also moved other groups out of their technology silos, such as IT planning and architecture.

To understand these actions, we need to consider that, in each case, these groups were separated or extracted from the infrastructure and application verticals for many of the same basic reasons. Each group has an enterprise mandate, but it is often found that they struggle with a conflict of interest by being placed within either an application or an infrastructure group with a vertical or domain focus. To resolve this issue, organizations have structurally removed them from their traditional positions in the organizational chart, and have created their own separate management groups specifically focused on servicing the enterprise.

An unattractive alternative to this approach would be to create multiple redundant groups in every management silo, offering the same services, where, in some cases, they actually compete with each other for business. One alternative to completely centralizing a shared professional service, such as project management, is to create a federated model where a small central project management office centrally manages a distributed or federated resource pool. The PMO provides a single point of contact, and receives, co-ordinates and sources all requests for project managers from the resource pool of project managers across the various IT domains.

The inherent conflict of interest, removal of redundancy and the goal of enterprise Service Delivery that has driven these changes, in groups such as Project, Security and Risk Management, are the same challenges faced by the Service Management roles of Service and Process Ownership.

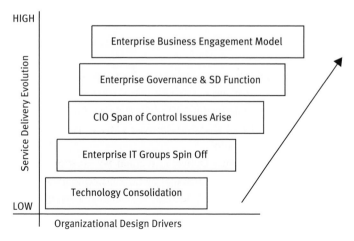

Figure 1.12 – The evolving IT Service Organization

Based on these trends what can be observed occurring over time is the evolution of a third IT management silo that houses the enterprise Service Delivery and governance functions of IT management.

Typically, we see a natural progression of an organization's move to a Service Delivery model through a very predictable sequence.

1) cost pressures or legislation force consolidation of key services and functions
2) enterprise IT functions such as a PMO, Security, HR and IT Finance are created or consolidated as separate management structures
3) initially, these groups report to either the application or infrastructure executives
4) organizational or authority challenges force consideration that these functions actually belong outside each of these silos; the individual groups are transitioned as stand-alone functions
5) for a time, these separate functions report directly to the CIO; however, as more and more enterprise functions are defined, a span of control issue is created with too many direct reports to the CIO
6) to resolve the span of control issue and the organizational challenges, a new Senior Executive is established and is given the mandate of IT Governance or Service Delivery which includes the oversight of these enterprise functions, including ITSM
7) eventually, the Service Delivery organizations represent the enterprise IT function to the business and facilitate the primary business engagement processes between the customer, the IT service owners and IT engagement roles supplied by SLM; this process is front-ended by the IT Service Catalog

Based on this set of observable evolutionary steps, the following illustration presents a model of an example end-state Service Delivery organizational design. It is interesting to note that many organizations have begun to follow this path without perhaps realizing why.

Implementing a Service Delivery structure such as this presents the following benefits:

- consolidation of key IT services with an enterprise IT mandate
- supporting the infrastructure and application groups in their goal of IT domain optimization, while at the same time establishing the governance and ownership structures required to support IT Service Delivery across both internal and external providers
- removing potential conflicts of interest from IT groups with an enterprise mandate which find themselves within traditional vertical IT silos
- establishing a core IT Governance and Service Delivery function which supports the ability to selectively outsource elements of the application and infrastructure silos
- providing IT with a single face and business engagement model with the business customer
- focusing a key element of the IT organization on Service Delivery based on managed clear business requirements
- ensuring that IT manages against three types of measures:

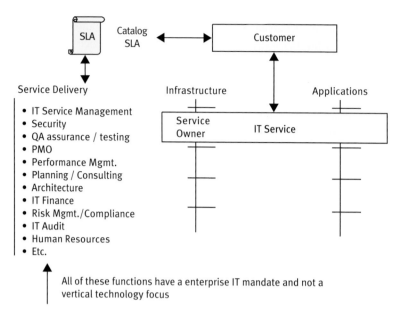

Figure 1.13 – An example of end-state Service Delivery organizational design

- Business Service Metrics
- Technology Metrics
- Process Improvement Metrics

■ 1.13 Impact on IT Outsourcing

The use of external service providers is an emerging trend in the business of supplying IT services. The Service Delivery function that has been described in this document is especially critical when a decision has been made to outsource key elements of the IT Organization.

External business legislation has made it clear that, while the execution of IT technology functions can be outsourced, governance and accountability can never be given away to an external provider. Ownership, measurement and oversight of continuous improvement must be kept within the internal IT function. For this reason, the new Service Delivery function represented in Figure 1.13 is necessary to enable IT outsourcing options while maintaining governance, ownership and measurement internally

The use of external providers can range from highly-defined contracts that 'out-task' relatively small blocks of service, to full 'soup to nuts' managed services contracts, in which a customer monitors service provisions and alters their characteristics in real time. Outsourcing individual technology functions is a more common activity than outsourcing an organization's entire IT infrastructure and management. Outsourcing literature now places less importance on hard cash cost savings and more importance on business benefits, the soft cash (or qualitative) savings, and the strategic purposes of outsourcing selective pieces of the IT environment for just-in-time (JIT) resource availability.

The complexity that this model presents makes the creation of a strong and empowered Service Delivery function all the more compelling. IT must present a transparent and unified Service Delivery capability to its business customer regardless of which parts of the technology function are swapped in or out to internal or external providers.

1.14 Global Process Governance Considerations

Due to the size and complexity of the global operations, it will be critical to implement a scaled governance and ownership model in order to build and manage the processes on an ongoing improvement basis.

Key roles that will need to be formalized include:

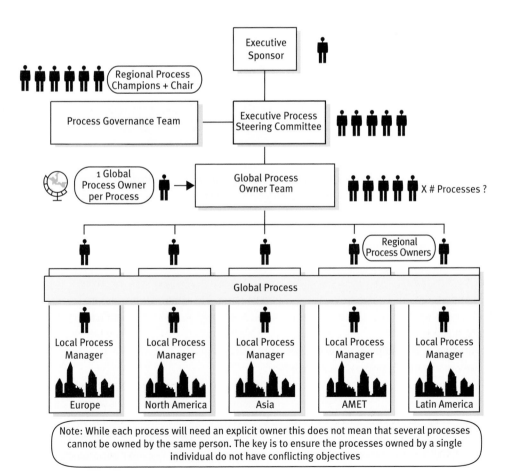

Figure 1.14: Key roles for organizational governance

■   1.15 Executive Sponsor

The Executive Sponsor makes the process re-engineering happen. This individual is a senior executive with enough authority to lead an organization through a major change initiative. The Executive Sponsor kicks off the organization's process improvement efforts at an executive level and appoints the Executive Steering Board, which is tasked to oversee and approve the global program. Demonstrated commitment and participation from the sponsor is necessary for a process re-engineering project to be successful. In his book, *Leading Change*, Harvard Professor John Kotter illustrates that a sponsor's role is comprised of 25% management and 75% leadership.

The re-engineering sponsor can demonstrate leadership through timely participation and by building a culture and global governance structure that will ensure long term success. Explicit messages that a sponsor sends to the organization about the change initiative include:

- What does it mean?
- Why we are doing it?
- How we are going about it, and what will it take?

■   1.16 Executive Steering Committee

The Executive Steering Committee provides the leadership and approvals to launch, fund and guide specific project initiatives within the structure of the global process initiative. Charter sign-off and project change management is approved by this group, which includes representation from the various global regions. While this steering committee is critical for the successful execution of the global program, they will be equally critical in maintaining the ongoing health and welfare of the global processes. To this end, the existence of the Executive Steering Committee must be extended beyond the lifespan of the implementation program, and they must assist in sustaining the ongoing development, management and improvement of IT service management. After the program has concluded, this group is typically required to meet on a quarterly basis:

- for periodic review meetings, for approval of large organizational process and technology changes relating to regional process compliance, multi-regional financial expenditure and tool issues
- to support the global process governance team and global Process Owners in facilitation of organizational process escalation issues

■   1.17 Process Governance Team

The Global Process Governance team should be made up of regional process champions whose role is to provide advice and knowledge transfer to the Process Owners within their respective regions. These champions should understand ITIL at an advanced level and be able to provide guidance on the integration of processes at an activity and technology level. Additionally, the champions should understand how other complementary models such as COBIT, the Capability Maturity Model (CMM), and the Application Services Library (ASL) connect with and support the infrastructure practices described in ITIL. This small team of internal regional advisors will report to the Process Executive Management Committee and ensure overall compliance and integration of the global processes.

Governance responsibilities include:

- establishing the effectiveness of process interfaces, ensuring that they are operating as a whole
- ensuring a coherent and comprehensive approach to the design and implementation of processes across the organization to increase efficiency and minimize cost
- monitoring the performance of policies and KPIs to ensure the fulfillment of strategic objectives
- developing and managing a global management dashboard for reporting regional and global process KPIs to the executive sponsor and steering committee
- identifying and co-ordinating global continuous process improvement initiatives
- recommending changes to processes or services as needed

1.18 Global Process Owners

Best practices clearly indicate that Process Ownership should reside with a single individual to ensure clear accountability. On a global scale, this typically means that a tiered Process Ownership structure needs to be put in place to balance accountability with regional and local process execution.

The recommended approach for the global organization is to have each region identify a regional Process Owner for a single process or a limited set of collaborative processes. This Process Owner will participate on a peer team comprised of other regional representatives for the management of the processes under their control. While this team is essentially a team of global peers, it is highly recommended that a single individual be named as the global owner or chair for a specific process, with accountability to the process governance committee and executive steering group for escalation and communication activities.

While the global Process Owner has accountability for a single process or limited set of collaborative processes, it is beneficial for the various global Process Owners to meet periodically to address process integration and technology issues.

During the phase of process deployment, the global Process Owners will participate as the regional representatives and stakeholders. Each regional Process Owner will be responsible for initiating and guiding regional projects to implement the global processes within their specific regions. This requirement infers that a regional Process Owner will need to have sufficient resources, funding and political ability to effect change in their regions. The assignment of a junior resource to this role would be a risk to the overall global process program.

■ 1.19 Local process managers and co-ordinators

Due to regional size, complexity, political challenges and resource availability, the daily tasks of executing the processes are often delegated to process managers and co-ordinators. Due to these factors, the organization will need to review the assignment of process managers and/or co-ordinators. Typical daily activities of a process manager or co-ordinator are as follows:

Process Manager:

The Process Manager has accountability for a process within a specific local or organizational structure, and participates in both the design and execution of the process as part of the Process Management Team. The Process Manager is responsible for the operation of the defined and agreed process for their respective area, including:

- ensuring resources are allocated to the process
- ensuring it interfaces with all other relevant processes
- setting targets, processing audits, conducting efficiency reviews
- participating in the process review committee
- participating in the design / re-design of the process
- communicating the process to the process co-ordinators in their respective areas
- monitoring the KPIs and management metrics for their respective area

Process Co-ordinator (Operational Daily Focus):

Under the guidance of the Process Manager, the Co-ordinator is responsible for:

- executing the defined and agreed process for their respective area
- communicating relevant process information and issues to their respective process manager
- executing the process' administrative tasks and promoting the process at the support group level
- creating metrics and KPI reports
- liaising with (operational) IT staff to gain acceptance of the process and seeking feedback for process improvement
- ensuring compliance to follow the process
- maintaining process documentation

1.20 Education recommendations

This section represents a suggested level of ITIL education, in accordance with the proposed model of Process Ownership and governance.

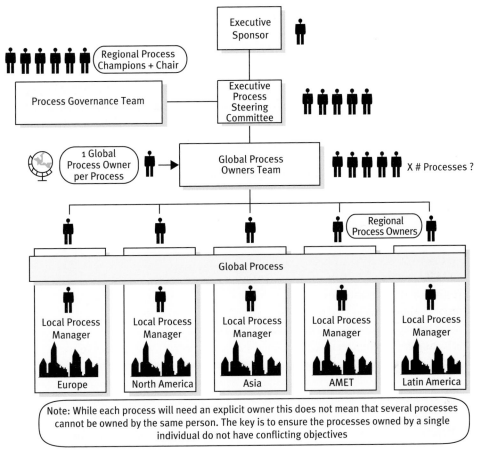

Figure 1.15: Key roles for Process Ownership and Governance

1.21 ITIL overviews

It is highly recommended that each person within the IT organization receives a high-level ITIL overview. The level and detail of overviews can be customized in accordance with the daily participation in Service Management processes:

- two hour overview – infrequent – irregular involvement
- four hour overview – occasional – regular involvement
- one-day overview – frequent involvement

The ITIL overview is designed with the intention of providing an introduction to the ITIL framework. Maximum class size is larger than a certification class, and is best suited for large-scale awareness programs for the general IT population. Careful consideration should be given to those people who fit into the 'frequent involvement' category. It is often more advantageous and has a greater personal benefit for these individuals to attend the two-day ITIL Foundation course.

1.22 Executive overview and executive strategic workshops

The executive level of ITIL awareness is typically represented by either a two or four hour ITIL overview targeted for the executive audience, or by the delivery of the one-day strategic workshop.

The key differences between these two sessions are that the overview is designed as a general awareness session of the ITIL process framework, while the workshop has been created to provide ITIL awareness in context with additional subjects.

The following areas should be covered in an Executive Workshop:

*   an ITIL overview
*   cultural and organizational change
*   process improvement best practices
*   program and project management recommendations
*   selecting enabling technologies
*   developing and setting up a measurement framework for continuous improvement
*   brainstorming / troubleshooting session on issues specific to the company
*   the association of IT governance and legislation with Service Management

Key Roles:

*   Executive Sponsor
*   Executive Steering Committee
*   Process Champions and Governance Team

1.23 ITIL Foundations Certification

It is highly recommended that anyone involved in the Process Ownership model - other than the executive members - be required to attend and pass the ITIL Foundation course. This is a prerequisite course for further ITIL study and certification, and should be made a mandatory requirement for those individuals tasked with the co-ordination, management, ownership or governance of the global Service Management processes.

Key Roles:

- process co-ordinators
- process managers
- Process Owners
- global Process Owners
- global process champions

1.24 ITIL and ITSM Practitioners

The Practitioner level courses are intended for individuals tasked with the implementation, ongoing management and continuous improvement of specific or collective processes. For this reason, it is highly recommended that the following roles be identified for Practitioner level education and certification.

Key Roles:

- process managers
- Process Owners
- global Process Owners
- global process champions

1.25 Summary

The influence of an on going Service Delivery organization is comprehensive and integrates with practically all areas of IT. For most organizations, the application of new structures, standards and controls described in this book will take time to fully realize. At a practical level, it is important to realize that the movement and organizational change requirements to accomplish this task will have to occur in a step fashion.

Technology management is focused on the cost-optimization of technology domains as uniquely managed silos, whereas a Service Management organization is *also* concerned with how technology components are assembled into services and their successful delivery. It is important to understand that the establishment of service and process structures within an organization must also be supported with the creation and empowerment of ownership and management roles and KPIs.

Without these roles, the work to define services and processes has been largely done in vain, with no lasting ability to survive or improve Service Delivery and Service Management for IT customers.

2

IT Governance Unraveled

Introduction

The role of IT governance is changing in the face of business pressures and international legislation. The enforcement of IT controls and the implementation of accepted best practices and standards, such as ITIL®, CMM, and ISO 17799, are no longer remaining optional. Additionally, Control Objectives for Information and Related Technology (COBIT) is fast becoming a global standard for defining the framework of best practices for IT governance.

■ 2.1 IT Governance Definition:

According to the IT Governance Institute (ITGI) the definition of IT governance is as follows:

> *"IT Governance is the responsibility of the board of directors and executive management. It is an integral part of Enterprise Governance and consists of the leadership, organizational structures and processes that ensure that the organization's IT sustains and extends the organization's strategies and objectives."*

Source: Board Briefing On IT Governance, IT Governance Institute, 2003

The scope of responsibility of IT governance has been summarized by the ITGI as covering the following areas:

1. **Strategic Alignment:** with focus on aligning IT strategy and planning.
2. **Value Delivery:** optimizing service delivery, processes, quality and speed with expense.
3. **Risk Management:** addressing and ensuring the safe guarding of IT assets.
4. **Resource Management:** optimizing knowledge, IT environments, structures and establishing accountability.
5. **Performance Management:** monitoring IT services and tracking project delivery.

In order to accomplish these responsibilities, the conventional approach to IT governance is expanding beyond its traditional boundaries. This chapter will define the three key activities of IT Governance (establishing, monitoring and directing).

■ 2.2 Activities of IT governance

As stated at the beginning of this book, it is the nature of ideas, structures and functions to mature and change over time as the needs placed upon these concepts evolve. This is also true of the area of IT governance. The IT industry as a whole is undergoing a transformation from an industry largely shaped by the leadership and personalities of individual IT executives and vendors, to one that is becoming more defined, homogeneous, codified and regulated.

Until recently, each organization's IT functions, controls and processes were largely defined by the company culture and by the personalities of a series of Chief Information Officers (CIOs) and technical heroes who have led the IT organization through its growth over the last two decades. Based on this observation, it is not surprising to find that the practices and definitions of IT governance differ significantly between organizations. In some companies, an IT engineering and architectural group is responsible for the function of IT governance; however, this function is typically limited to the establishment of standards on hardware and software being brought into the IT environment. Typically, little is done in the way of measuring compliance or in providing education and assistance in the deployment of these standards. In other organizations, governance takes on the pure function of audit and policing. In these companies, limited guidance is provided on what, who and how. For the most part, the focus is based on ensuring that bad behavior is caught and punished rather than on the promotion of positive activity.

While each of these elements plays a part in the concept of governance, there is a more holistic view of IT governance emerging around the world, which encompasses elements of the scenarios described above, but goes much further in assisting in the development of strategies and direction for the IT organization.

This recent formalization of the concept, scope and role of IT governance is largely being driven by a series of legislative initiatives emerging around the world, relating to **Enterprise (Business) Governance**. These legislations focus on the duties of public and private companies to act in a manner of trust in relation to the maintenance and security of customer data and the publishing of accurate financial information. This change in view is based on the understanding that core business processes, transactions and data are directly linked to the IT services and systems which store and publish this information, as well as the IT structures and processes which control and support these systems. As a result, governments around the world are requiring IT organizations to become accountable and auditable for their IT practices. To achieve this objective, a global movement is evolving to formalize the scope of IT governance as a consistent model agnostic of industry sector and geographic location. In short, IT is moving away from a model of informal and ad-hoc controls towards a regulated model of codes and practices. Many industry analysts eagerly adopt the term of utility computing. However, consider that, when any service truly enters the space of being a utility, it becomes more important to focus on the risk of not having it, than on the strategic advantage it provides over and above a competitor. The very nature of becoming a utility requires our industry to become more formal in its controls and practices. To this end, COBIT is being adopted as an accepted governance framework to provide this definition and auditable model.

Establishing: Frameworks such as COBIT can assist in providing a scope as to which areas IT governance covers. However, it is important to keep in mind the principles that a governance model should cover when effectively deployed in an organization. In short, IT governance is primarily concerned with supporting the objectives of Enterprise Governance and in doing so, should **establish** the basis for sound and aligned provisioning of services to the business customer. The ultimate driver for good governance should be in relation to meeting business goals and complying with regulatory and risk management issues facing Enterprise Governance.

Monitoring: The establishment of standards is of limited value if structures and measurements are not put into place to **monitor** the effectiveness and compliance to the standards being deployed to meet the business needs. In order to address the issues of facilitating organizational and cultural change in support of IT governance, it is critical to develop a culture of continuous improvement and measurement. The development of enterprise level IT dashboards, to regularly report on the health of the IT controls and processes in support of the established standards, is a major factor of effective governance. Due to the fact that processes and controls are cross-functional in nature, these dashboards must take an enterprise view of the activities which are occurring in IT that is not limited by the typical organizational silos. The simple truth is, *'what gets measured gets done'*. However, without the development of a mature and balanced measurement framework, a company can also suffer from the converse statement, *'be careful that what is measured does not become the only thing that is done.'*

Directing: Based on the observations and inputs of monitoring, it is important that raw data and metrics be turned into analysis and information that can be used to identify significant deficiencies or material weaknesses within an organization's structures, processes and controls. From this information, IT governance must **direct** and assist the organization in where and how to close gaps and mitigate risks. Gaps and risks can be identified, based on non-compliance to existing standards, or the need to adhere to new ones, based on new business or regulatory pressures.

From the arguments outlined in this chapter, it is clear that organizations will need to develop a formal and strong IT governance function complete with roles, processes, measures and controls. Due to the complexities of balancing business needs with changing legislative requirements, there is an increasing need to develop this discipline as a formal and ongoing capability within IT organizations of all sizes. As a concept and function, IT governance has the potential of drastically changing the face of IT from the one that has been known for the last twenty years.

Directing:	Continuous Improvement: Process/Standards Structures/Systems		Research & Recommendation of new – Standards/Best Practice – Technology – Structures/Resources		
Managing:	Risk Identification & Mgmt.	External Legislation/ Regulation & Audit output requirements		Monitoring Compliance Data Analysis Reporting	
Establishing:	Business & Legislation requirements (Finance/Privacy)	Standards Best Practice Mgmt. Models	Ownership: – Process – Systems – Data	Mgmt. Dashboards – KPIs – Maturity Models	
Responsibilities: ITGI	Alignment of IT with the business	Value Delivery of IT	Management of Risks	Resource Management	Performance Management

Table 2.1: IT governance – responsibilities and activities

■ 2.3 Establishing

Of the three activities required to support the responsibilities of IT governance, the establishment of oversight, accountability and adoption of standards and measurement models is the best understood and most widely executed activity. IT governance is ultimately responsible for assisting in the crafting of an enterprise level strategic road-map for what the IT organization should look like in relation to organizational structures, processes and technologies. While this includes technology standards, it also covers areas which pertain to the adoption of recognized best practice standards for all IT areas. Also, in keeping with the increased focus of accountability, IT governance is also concerned with developing an enterprise level ownership and accountability model which explicitly defines single owners for IT systems, processes and services, as well as the storage and transit of data.

Governance vs Management

It is important at this point to draw the distinction between the role of IT Governance versus the execution of the established vision and direction. IT Governance is responsible for setting vision and direction while establishing effective controls to ensure compliance to its directives. The fulfillment or execution of the governance requirements is the activity of management. However, it is important not to make too fine a distinction between the aspects of Governance versus Management, because one without the other cannot be supported. Establishing an IT Governance vision and model without execution is as ineffective at meeting Enterprise

Governance requirements as not having them at all. From this perspective one could argue that IT Governance has the final accountability for establishing direction, delegating execution and measurement of its principals.

2.3.1   Business priorities, requirements, objectives

The scope of IT governance is comprehensive and covers practically all areas within IT. For most organizations, the application of new structures, standards and controls will take time to fully realize. At a practical level, it is important to realize that the movement and organizational change requirements to accomplish this task will have to occur in a step fashion. For this reason, IT governance is required to provide guidance on the prioritization of which activities need to be addressed. Multiple inputs must be considered to build this prioritized model, such as:

* business drivers
* enterprise governance requirements
* risk management priorities
* regulatory requirements
* organizational change and cultural considerations
* technology status
* process dependencies
* existing structures
* opportunities for quick wins

This prioritization exercise will ultimately resolve itself into an ongoing assessment and service improvement program. These assessments will produce a plan to be considered as a key input into the annual IT strategic planning and budgeting processes executed by IT management.

2.3.2   External legislation requirements

Around the world, governments are legislating requirements relating to the management and reporting of corporate data, which has a direct implication on how the data is managed within the IT systems which manipulate it. Along with these rules come explicit requirements for digital data storage, retention, transit and access policies. How transactional data is stored, and which business and IT roles are permitted to have explicit types of access is a key consideration of IT governance. Additionally, the general IT processes which control and support the business applications and data are equally coming under the scrutiny of regulatory requirements.

The challenge facing corporations is that regulatory requirements are being defined at multiple levels of government. Laws dealing with privacy and financial legislation are being established at a global, national, and regional level, which, at times, contradict each other. Companies which operate across any form of political boundary are required to be aware of how legislation changes in each new political environment. One key example of this is where privacy legislation for Canadian-based companies is contradicted by the US Patriot Act, when that data resides within the United States. This example is applicable when a Canadian company outsources data management to a US-based legal entity. By law, the customer data stored within the US site can be subpoenaed by the Bureau of Intelligence based on legislation formulated under Homeland Security.

Table 2.2 provides a sample of the types of legislation which apply directly to IT management of systems and data:

• Privacy & Security	• Finance
– Personal Information Protection Electronic Document Act (PIPEDA)	– Sarbanes Oxley (US)
– US Patriot Act \Homeland Security (Critical Infrastructure)	– FFIEC US Banking Standard
– Personal Health Information Protection Act (PHIPA)	– Basel II (World Bank)
– Health Insurance Portability and Accountability Act (HIPAA)	– Turnbull Report (UK)
– SEC Rules 17a -3 & 17 a4 re: Securities Transaction Retention	– Canadian Bill 198 (MI 52-109 & 52-111)
– Gramm-Leach Bliley Act (GLBA) privacy of financial information	– CIRCULAR A-123 (US Gov.)
– Children's Online Privacy Protection Act	– J-Sox (Japan)
– Clinger-Cohen Act (US Gov.)	• Other International IT Models
– Federal Information Security Mgmt. Act (FISMA)	– Corporate Governance for ICT DR 04198 (Australia)
– Freedom of Information & Protection of Privacy (FOIPOP) BC Gov	– IntragobQuality Effort (Mexico)
– FDA Regulated IT Systems	– Medical Information System Development (Medis-DC) (Japan)
– Freedom Of Information Act	– Authority for IT in the Public Administration (AIPA) (Italy)
– Americans with Disabilities Act, Sec. 508 (website accessibility)	– Principles of accurate data processing supported accounting systems (GDPdu& GoBS) (Germany)
– Family Education Rights & Privacy Act (FERPA) (Higher Education)	– European Privacy Directive (Safe Harbor Framework)

Table 2.2: The IT Legislation Minefield

In summary, regulatory requirements are becoming too complex to understand without a formal function of IT governance to examine the application of these laws and provide guidance on how and where to apply controls that ensure corporate compliance from an IT perspective. Not to do so places the business at risk of litigation, financial penalties and perhaps, most seriously, brand and reputation loss. Each of these elements represents a critical impact against the company's ability to generate revenue or fulfill its mandate.

2.3.3 Standards, best practice and management models

As part of the movement towards a more regulated approach to the delivery of IT services, there is a growing recognition that there is benefit and perhaps even a requirement to apply internationally recognized best practice standards to the management of IT. The identification, selection and adoption of these standards is a part of the developing role of IT governance. Where models such as COBIT can provide a scope of which elements need to be in place, it is necessary to select a strategic collection of best practice frameworks covering the various areas of IT management to provide the detail needed to understand the requirements at a level of detail that can be executed.

"Until recently the development of controls were voluntary and based on a wide variety of internal control frameworks. To improve consistency and quality, the SEC has mandated the use of a recognized internal control framework that is established by a body or group that has followed due-process procedures, including the broad distribution of the framework for public comment. In its final rules, specific reference is made to the recommendations of the Committee of Sponsoring Organizations of the Treadway Commission, otherwise known as COSO." ~ IT CONTROL OBJECTIVES FOR SARBANES-OXLEY published by the IT Governance Institute

Commonly used non–propriety models being adopted to satisfy governance requirements:

- Application lifecycle management: Capability Maturity Model (CMM)
- Application maintenance and support: Application Services Library (ASL)
- Service Management: Information Technology Infrastructure Library (ITIL)
- Security management: ISO 17799
- Computer operations and data / LAN: Electronic Telecommunications Map (ETOM)
- Quality management: Six Sigma / ISO
- Project management : PMI or PRINCE2

While there is no explicit regulatory requirement to adhere to a specific best practice framework, there is an unprecedented movement occurring towards these models. Organizations are beginning to recognize the inherent benefits of adopting a recognized best practice framework. In addition, it can also be argued that there is an inherent need to provide an auditable set of controls which can be recognized and verified by an outside agent.

The following model provides a graphical view of the relationships between legislation, corporate risk management (COSO), the COBIT IT governance model and best practice frameworks and standards.

At the very least, the implementation of an enterprise level IT governance function can assist in bringing disparate and currently unconnected improvement activities within the

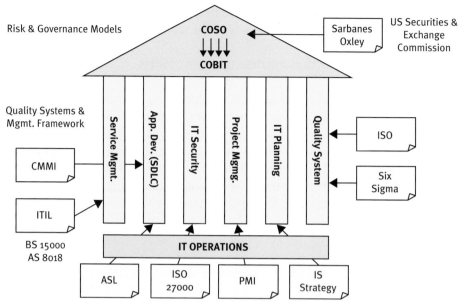

Figure 2.1: IT Governance Model

organization into alignment with each other. This activity alone will provide better use of limited resources and explore the intrinsic relationships between the models.

2.3.4 Ownership (processes, services, systems and data)

A core element at the base of governance is the establishment of accountability and the mapping of explicit responsibility for the deployment and ongoing management of controls and standards. Ultimately, a single owner needs to be established at the right level of the organization to effectively gain political consensus and cross-organizational compliance. Most organizations face a significant shift in culture and structure to achieve what, in effect, is major organizational change. The end goal of this objective is to establish a single owner who is accountable for each major element involved in the development, operations and provisioning of services to the business customer. The concept of ownership extends to services, IT systems, portfolios of systems, data ownership and Process Ownership. The development of the concept of a single point of ownership is a critical success factor in ensuring the consistency of controls and process execution across disparate groups and functional silos. This is further complicated when the functional silos differ in organizational structure and culture, as well as in geographical and business focus.

The role of ownership extends beyond the concept of accountability to encompass quality assurance and organizational awareness, as well as the concept of political advocacy.

For larger organizations, this can mean the development of a sophisticated hierarchical management and reporting structure which establishes ownership at a local, regional and enterprise level. The activities and roles of such a structure are essentially a matrix-based model which is difficult to implement and is likely be new to the culture of the current IT organization.

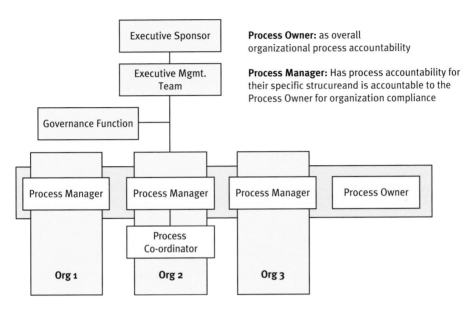

Figure 2.2: Typical roles in a large scale implementation

2.3.5 Management Dashboards (KPIs, KGIs, maturity models)

Many organizations recognize the impact that measures have on performance. However, the development of a culture of measurement is rarely thought of as an essential part of their strategy. For example, executives may introduce new strategies and innovative business processes such as ITIL, intended to achieve optimization and improved efficiencies, and then continue to focus on the same short-sighted financial-based metrics that have been in use for years. Not only is it important to introduce new measures to monitor new goals, but also to question whether or not the former measures still have bearing and validity against the new initiatives.

In order to measure the health and maturity of a control, process or system, organizations need to develop a balanced or multi-dimensional framework of Key Performance Indicators (KPIs). The multi-dimensional aspect of these KPIs is very important, since any limited combination of the indicators below might lead the organization to believe incorrectly that the control or process is operating maturely and efficiently.

By definition, a key performance indicator should be a chosen metric which represents a key health or maturity indicator of the element being measured. A relatively new term introduced by COBIT is Key Goal Indicator (KGI). By definition, a KGI is a specific measurement that provides information as to whether the control or process is actually achieving the intended goal. Another foundation element of IT governance is the establishment of an enterprise measurement framework that can be used to measure consistently any process or control. If KPIs are developed in accordance with an established framework, they can then be rolled up to an enterprise level to provide a corporate dashboard, relating to the activities under the influence of IT governance.

The following four KPI quadrants represent a balanced approach for consistently developing KPI dashboards, by which the owner can determine the health of the activity, process or control being measured:

Value: reports or surveys, to measure the effectiveness and perceived value and effectiveness of the control or process to the stakeholders and users.

Quality: quality indicators are typically activity-based, and are established to measure the quality of individual or key activities, as opposed to the effectiveness of the entire process against its stated goal.

Performance / Throughput: time-sensitive metrics which are established under this KPI category measure the average process throughput or cycle time (eg metrics to capture the speed and performance of the stated process goal and output).

Compliance: compliance seeks to measure the percentage of deployment or acceptance that a control or process enjoys across the IT organization. A process may have a perceived value, good quality and adequate throughput, but still be seen as immature if only a small percentage of the organization complies.

In short, KPIs are required to answer the following questions:

Compliance: Are we doing it?

Performance: How fast or slow are we doing it?

Quality: How well are we doing it?

Value: Is what we are doing making a difference?

■ 2.4 Monitoring

As necessary as it is to establish controls and standards, if they are not measured, analyzed and reported on, they will simply have little or no effect. As mentioned earlier, many organizations have established groups which set standards but do little else to assist with their implementation, let alone monitoring whether or not they are actually accomplished.

In order to be effective, the IT governance function must play an active role in monitoring, measuring and analyzing key IT data. This activity may take several forms:

- the creation of an IT corporate management dashboard
- the development and execution of an IT risk management process
- the co-ordination of periodic comprehensive assessments

Each of these elements will provide input to influence the annual IT planning and budgeting process.

2.4.1 Risk management

A risk is the possibility of suffering a loss, and risk management is essentially the process of identifying how IT risks relating to internal as well as external factors can affect the business in a negative way. A major focus within the regulatory requirements of IT governance is the development and deployment of a comprehensive risk management process as an enterprise-wide discipline. As with the development of a KPI framework, a consistent model for identifying, classifying and monitoring risks needs to be deployed across the organization, and rolled up to the IT governance function for prioritization and escalation purposes.

Risks can be classified by source, impact or exposure and should have an appropriate mitigation and perhaps contingency plan in place, based on the likelihood of occurrence and the exposure that it brings to the business.

In the past, risk management activities have been largely left up to each functional area to execute. In most cases, this results in a fragmented approach to identifying risks within a specific functional silo. Each functional manager is left to their own devices to manage risks within their group, usually based on an informal and ad hoc approach. However, based on the interdependencies of technical areas, a silo-based approach is not adequate to understand the complex relationships and dependencies between environments which can adversely affect service delivery and ultimately, the integrity of business transactions and data. IT governance must assume the task of establishing a formal risk management process, and also assume the responsibility of the roll-up of risks from each functional area to provide the appropriate enterprise view and consideration.

In summary, the IT organization has great potential to facilitate business goals. However, failures in IT controls and processes also have the potential essentially to disable business beyond recovery, from a legal reputation perspective as well as regards technical capacity. As a result, it is absolutely critical that the ongoing monitoring of risks be established within an IT governance function.

2.4.2   Facilitating audit and external legislation requirements

Along with the regulatory aspect of IT governance comes the legislative requirement to establish the burden of proof that all is as it should be. These exercises typically assume the form of annual or periodic audits by both internal as well as external groups. For some organizations, these activities may occur numerous times throughout the period of a year. In order to facilitate these requirements without undue impact to the business of providing IT services, these requirements need to be co-ordinated by a central function which has oversight of all IT.

The central view and management of these activities is important, both from a scheduling perspective and for the proactive identification of absent controls and missing evidence, as well as the co-ordination of gap remediation activities. Much like risk management, this cannot be effectively managed at a silo or functional level, but must be co-ordinated from an enterprise IT governance perspective.

In short there are two primary goals to accomplish:

1. facilitate and co-ordinate the sometimes numerous audit requirements, while protecting the organization from assessment fatigue
2. proactively identify and remediate gaps in audit requirements prior to an external assessment, with enough lead time to provide sufficient material evidence to pass a period of time review

2.4.3   Monitoring, analyzing and reporting

"Measurements should induce the parts to do what is good for the whole, and measurements should direct managers to those parts that need their attention."

Source: Eli. Goldratt

Organizations measure for a variety of reasons, but at the base of all the activity and energy expended on measurement, there are really only two fundamental questions.

Where are we now in relation to where we want to be?

Are we improving, standing still or getting worse?

IT dashboards, comprehensive maturity assessments and external audits are all basically tools to answer these two fundamental questions. While it is true that each functional group and process will generate their own metrics and management reports, these need to be rolled up with analytics to an IT enterprise level, which considers the disparate data sources as a collection of connected information. Essentially, there are limited resources and financing available to correct the areas which are most needing attention. Resource prioritization and planning, in relation to areas covered by IT governance, must be done at a strategic level.

■ 2.5 Directing

From the arguments laid out in this chapter, one could assume that IT governance is crossing into the realm of IT management. While it is true that governance has a responsibility for establishing, monitoring and directing key areas of the IT organization, it remains in the hands of IT executives and managers to approve, adjust and deploy the controls, processes and activities within the organization. The premise of IT governance is to provide strategic guidance and input for the IT executive and management functions to act upon, based on the key inputs established earlier in this chapter.

With this in mind, it is logical to conclude that IT governance provides ongoing direction to the IT organization based on the monitoring and analysis. This direction should be based on the identification of opportunities, risks, gaps and issues of non-compliance. Based on this premise, it is important to understand that the function of IT governance is to provide strategic direction in the following key areas:

Continuous improvement of:

• existing structures, controls, standards, processes and systems

Research and recommendation for:

• new structures, controls, standards, processes and systems

■ 2.6 Summary

As the IT industry matures and moves towards a utility-based model of service provisioning, companies around the world are transforming themselves in support of a competition model that is based on information management. The ability to exploit intangible assets such as business processes and data has become a far more decisive competitive advantage than the ability to manage physical assets. To accomplish this objective, the concept and function of IT governance explored in this chapter is critical to achieve the organizational, cultural and process changes required to meet this challenge.

3

The External Managed Service Provider

3.1 Introduction

Business focused approaches for managing IT resources are highly valued in today's enterprise. As IT departments and organizations transition from technology to service-based management models, investment in a credible, best practice framework such as ITIL is becoming more important.

This increased importance is exemplified by the state of ITIL awareness. A recent survey of global IT professionals revealed that 71% of respondents rate best practice frameworks such as ITIL from critical to highly critical for ensuring the continued success of their organizations and about the same percentage are actively implementing the framework. This contrasts sharply with an earlier 2003 study that revealed 74% of respondents were not at all familiar with ITIL. These findings add to further support for ITIL from leading industry analysts, including Forrester and Gartner:

"2005 will be the year that ITIL goes mainstream – widespread adoption will continue through to 2008. At that point, ITIL will be set to become the de-facto best practice service delivery standard methodology that every IT department will have to adhere to."

Source: Forrester

"Fully adopting an IT service management strategy can cut an organization's cost of IT ownership by 50%."

Source: Gartner

There are three main reasons for ITIL's increased popularity:

1. on-going pressure to 'do more with less', creating a need to govern day-to-day operations
2. trends towards the definition and management of end-to-end services; this is represented by the development of an IT Service Catalog as well as SLAs that are focused on a complete IT service and its impact on the user experience rather than separate technology components or domains
3. changes in IT governance requiring IT to comply with recent legislation

An important aspect of the new legislation is the requirement for organizations to have consistent and formalized application controls as well as general controls across all IT functions, including areas outsourced to external partners. To achieve these goals, organizations are adopting ITIL to provide a framework for best practices, and, many of these organizations are taking this a step further by seeking out external partners who use complementary, compatible processes. These organizations want to share the same consistent, common language as they contract out and transition a specific area of their IT organization. Consequently, Managed Service Providers (MSPs) are facing mounting pressure from potential customers to demonstrate how their services align with ITIL best practices. This chapter aims to illustrate and describe the reasons for an MSP to adopt ITIL, as well as some of the pitfalls that an MSP might encounter in the current IT environment.

■ 3.2 Background on MSPs and ITIL

3.2.1 MSPs

The use of MSPs to enhance IT service offerings is complicated by the evolution of the outsourcing market and the wide range of services now available. Originally, outsourcing was used primarily to contract for data centre services and facilities management, as vendors provided economies of scale for mainframe use. In the 1980s, outsourcing expanded to include the goal of using only external resources and services to develop and manage all IT activities.

The primary motivations were:

• cost savings
• the desire to avoid or defer high risk capital investments in new technologies
• the necessity of greater agility in dealing with rapidly changing scalability requirements
• the need to focus on the core business processes of the organization

Now as indicated in the earlier chapter, outsourcing can range from highly-defined contracts that 'out-task' relatively small blocks of service to full 'soup to nuts' managed services contracts in which a customer monitors service provisions and alters their characteristics in real time.

Outsourcing individual business functions is a more common activity than outsourcing an organization's entire IT infrastructure and management. Outsourcing literature now places less importance on hard cash cost savings and more importance on business benefits, the soft cash (or qualitative) savings, and the strategic purposes of outsourcing selective pieces of the IT environment. IT leaders need to be able to match their specific needs with both the correct service and the correct MSP.

3.2.2 ITIL Best Practice Service Lifecycle Model

ITIL is a non-proprietary approach for managing IT services, developed in the 1980s by the Office of Government Commerce (OGC) in the United Kingdom. Now considered the de facto standard for managing a business focused, cost effective IT organization, the ITIL framework was recently redesigned from a process-led approach to a service lifecycle approach. This end-to-end view of how IT should be integrated with business strategy is at the heart of ITIL v3's five core volumes:

- Service Strategy which looks at overall business aims and expectations to ensure IT strategy maps back to them
- Service Design which starts with a set of new or changed business requirements and ends with the development of a solution designed to meet the documented needs of the business
- Service Transition which is concerned with managing change, risk and quality assurance and has an objective to implement service designs so that service operations can manage the services and infrastructure in a controlled manner
- Service Operation which is concerned with business as usual activities
- Continual Service Improvement which has an overall view of all other elements and looks for ways that the overall process and service provision can be improved

The ITIL Library is a set of books that guide business users through the planning, delivery and management of quality IT services. At a time of increasing dependence on IT, the series is an essential reference source for people responsible for managing the delivery of quality IT services; however, all staff delivering IT services will find the books useful. The books help them gain an understanding of the context of their work.

Today, ITIL represents more than books alone. It has generated an entire industry that includes:

- complimentary guidance
- training
- certification
- consulting
- software tools
- trade associations

3.2.3   Benefits of ITIL

Business profitability and stakeholder loyalty is dependent on the high availability, dependability, security and performance of IT services. This fact has made the relative maturity or immaturity of IT management highly visible. Many companies state that due to the rapidly changing nature of their business and the pressure from competition to become more cost-effective while still achieving the same or greater profits and output, they do not have time or resources to apply to IT process improvement. This is short-sighted. In fact, this is exactly the time when consistent and well-defined processes are the most critical to gain efficiencies in IT operations.

By improving the processes around IT, the organization can begin to:

- improve resource utilization
- be more competitive
- decrease rework
- eliminate redundant work
- improve upon project deliverables and time
- improve availability, reliability and security of mission critical IT services
- justify the cost of service quality
- provide services that meet business, customer and user demands
- integrate central business processes
- document and communicate roles and responsibilities in service provision
- learn from previous experience
- provide demonstrable performance indicators

In *An Introductory Overview of ITIL*, published in April 2004, the IT Service Management Forum (itSMF) states that the benefits of ITIL are twofold: It improves IT services while reducing delivery costs. Organizations have achieved savings by adopting a framework that supports IT governance; these include:

- more than 70% reduction in service downtime
- ROI up by more than 1,000 percent
- savings of nearly $200 million annually
- 50% reduction in new product cycles

3.2.4   ITIL as a standard

Until recently, ITIL discussions focused on it strictly as a best practices *framework* for IT Service Management. Discussions about certifications were focused on individuals rather than organizations.

In 2003 an international standard was published by the UK's British Standards Institution (BSI), entitled BS15000. This standard used ITIL's *Service Support* and *Service Delivery* processes and expanded upon ITIL in some areas. This was not an individual certification, but rather an institutional certification. As of November 2005, 42 organizations had received BS15000 certification worldwide. Nearly half of those were MSPs. The existence of a worldwide standard gives an MSP the ability to differentiate itself. BS15000 provided an internationally recognized *seal of approval* that states that the organization is running its IT operations according to all of the ITIL principles.

In 2005, BS15000 was transformed into ISO20000. ISO20000 was published in early 2006. Since the ISO certification is much more widely known and adopted than the BSI certifications, it is anticipated that the number of organizations seeking ISO20000 certification will expand rapidly.

3.2.5 Legislation and regulation

While IT governance is perceived as a 'really good idea' that would be 'nice to have', the same is not true of the legislative landscape that spans compliance, privacy, security and more.

High visibility corporate fraud (Enron, Tyco, Adelphia, etc.) has spawned far-reaching legislation such as Sarbanes-Oxley (SOX), introducing the element of compliance into today's IT operations. In many cases, for the first time, IT is being forced to manage their operations to comply with new and unfamiliar audit standards.

Additionally, the Internet, and the accompanying boom in online shopping and banking transactions, has spawned an ever-increasing list of privacy legislation in nearly every developed country.

The global threat of terrorism has created legislation with the opposite desire for information transparency (US Patriot Act). In some cases the privacy laws directly conflict. Specific industries such as banking and healthcare have their own laws in the areas of privacy, data retention and security. The US Government is beginning to enforce regulations (Clinger-Cohen and Circular A-123) that have been on the books for ten years or more.

3.2.6 COBIT

First published in 1995, COBIT began its life as an audit framework created by ISACA (Information Systems Audit and Control Association). Over the last decade it has been revised and consequently has become an IT governance and management framework. COBIT is the de facto standard for IT governance today.

In recent years, with the blessing of ISACA, the ITGI (IT Governance Institute) has taken over responsibility for the further development of COBIT. A revision (version 4.0) was implemented in 2006.

COBIT contains four domains:

1. monitoring: includes four key control objectives.
2. delivery and support: includes 13 key control objectives.
3. planning and organization: includes 11 key control objectives.
4. acquisition and implementation: includes six key control objectives.

3.2.7 SOX

Today, a publicly-traded US company that has more than US$75 million market capitalization is required to undergo an annual SOX audit. Section 404 of the SOX legislation requires that IT controls be audited as well.

The specific areas of IT that the SOX auditors focus on are:

- Data Access Control
- Separation of Duties
- Change Management
- Release Management
- Configuration Management
- the approvals, documentation and evidence of these processes

If an independent auditor finds problems in these or other areas of IT controls, they are required by law to publish 'material deficiencies' on the public audit report. Since this information is part of the due diligence process of any major investor, a lack of good IT processes can negatively impact a company's stock price.

This raises the question: 'What do the independent auditors use as a guide in assessing the controls of an IT organization?'

3.2.8 COBIT and SOX

There is no direct legislative requirement for SOX auditors to use COBIT as an audit baseline, nor is there a definitive set of controls for SOX or IT governance; however, ITGI has published guidance for the audit community on what might be the most relevant controls as they relate to a SOX audit. The twelve control objectives considered most relevant to SOX are:

1. acquire and develop application software
2. acquire technology infrastructure
3. develop and maintain policies and procedures
4. install and test application software and technology infrastructure
5. manage changes
6. define and manage service levels
7. manage third-party services

8. ensure systems security
9. manage the configuration
10. manage problems and incidents
11. manage data
12. manage operations

3.2.9 IT governance implications for MSPs

Into this turbulent sea of new standards and conflicting legislation comes the MSP.

Today, if the above publicly traded US company utilizes the services of an MSP to deliver all or part of their IT operations, then the MSP's processes will be audited with the same level of rigor as the original company. This is true even if the MSP itself is **not** publicly traded and / or is below US$75 million in market capitalization. Which processes are reviewed and the degree of scrutiny are at the auditor's discretion. Suddenly, and in some cases without warning, MSPs are facing multiple 'pass-through' audits generated from relationships with major clients. Audits can therefore increase the cost of doing business with those clients.

SOX highlights another troubling issue: data ownership and control. If a corporation or government agency (whether foreign or domestic) uses the services of a US-based MSP being audited, can the client's data be protected? If an MSP grants access to a client's data to an auditor or investigating government agency, must the MSP notify the client? Will the client have legal recourse if this situation is realized? These are the issues that are currently unresolved, but should be on the radar for both MSPs and their client organizations.

3.2.10 MSPs and SAS-70

The 'pass-through' audit concept has been around for years in the financial services area. To avoid costly, repetitive audits passing through from multiple clients, the American Institute of Certified Public Accountants (AICPA) developed a voluntary financial audit program called Statement on Auditing Standards No. 70, *Service Organizations*, otherwise known as a SAS-70. This is an international auditing standard that is widely recognized, because it signifies that a service organization has been through an in-depth audit of its control objectives and activities by an independent accounting and auditing firm within the last 12 months. A SAS-70 examination generally includes a review of the controls over information technology and related processes.

Increasingly, MSPs are being asked to provide proof of compliance from their customers through a SAS-70 Service Auditor's Report, either Type I or Type II. A SAS-70 Type I is a snapshot of the current state of an organization, while a SAS-70 Type II contains evidence of compliance over a specified period of time.

Other than cost, the only issue with a SAS-70 audit is that the MSP selects the areas of its own operation which are to be covered in the voluntary audit. These areas may differ significantly from those required by a SOX 'pass-through' audit.

3.2.11 ITIL and SAS-70

ITIL's processes can be harnessed to support a SAS-70 compliance program. Policies and compliance assertions can be directly supported by ITIL standards, processes, controls and work instructions. This reduces the need to use a 'point solution' approach where every compliance activity and response is an 'event' and a stand-alone effort which often produces a stand-alone result.

Consequently, a strong ITIL implementation can contribute to providing internal efficiencies for audits by reducing duplication of effort as well as providing compliance to the customer. Other benefits include:

combination of compliance with efficiency
protecting brand reputation and revenue streams
strengthening customer trust and overall relationship
marketplace differentiation
simplifying audit requests
establishing good business practice

3.2.12 Is there a SOX-70?

Unfortunately, there is not any generally accepted program at this time to reduce the number of annual 'pass-through' SOX audits that an MSP may be required to participate in. This is primarily because the legislation is new and the audit community has only had 12 months of experience conducting SOX audits. Indeed, a 'SOX-70' is exactly what is needed to accommodate the increasing demands of compliance placed on already stretched IT staffs.

3.2.13 Accountability

In closing this section, it is important to note that no matter how much is outsourced to an MSP, the accountability for all compliance lies with the original publicly traded company and its IT department. While the MSP may assume operational responsibility for a number of IT activities, under no circumstances can the MSP take over the legal or regulatory accountability for SOX or financial compliance.

This is as it should be. Legislation and compliance aside, the organization's internal IT department is always accountable for the successful delivery of efficient and cost effective IT services to the end customer, whether some or all of those services are outsourced.

■ 3.3 ITIL in an MSP environment

Unlike an internal IT service provider, an MSP has two specific views of ITIL: internal and external. With regard to their internal IT operations, MSPs are like any company with an internal IT department - they will benefit greatly from the establishment of clear, consistent, repeatable, documented and auditable IT processes. ITIL provides the framework and describes the processes. The MSP will not only reap internal operational benefits, they will also build expertise and credibility in the implementation of these processes with their customers. While the goals and definitions of ITIL's processes will not change in the external MSP environment, they will undoubtedly be implemented from a different point of view.

3.3.1 The Service Desk function and Service Support processes

Service Desk

ITIL defines the Service Desk as a customer's single point of contact (SPOC) for communication, not just with IT but any department providing services to the customer. The Service Desk is responsible for managing incidents to resolution and service requests to closure. In other words, within ITIL the Service Desk owns the customer relationship and is contacted first to respond to customer needs.

An MSP may offer a service to their customers called Service Desk. While this will be structured and defined by the specific contractual arrangement with the customer, an MSP would be wise to step back and look closely at the Service Desk goals.
These include:

- acting as a SPOC
- focusing on communication
- clear commitment to ownership
- measurability of service levels
- accountability for results

Incident Management

ITIL's Incident Management process has but one focus: restore service to the user as quickly as possible. The primary metric of Incident Management is time and the process encompasses every level of IT staff. While all incidents may be managed by the Service Desk, some incidents will be escalated to those with more expertise or authority. Depending on the range of services being provided, MSPs may be responsible only for incidents governing those specific services, creating the potential for confusing or non-existent hand-offs to the customer for root cause analysis.

MSPs may also be responsible for managing every incident in the enterprise, including incidents not reported to the Service Desk. It is essential for the MSP to define an incident, the severity and priority levels and their definitions, and the service levels expected for response, notification, customer communication, resolution and reporting. This will be made easier when the client and the MSP share a common language and common process definitions through ITIL.

Problem Management

ITIL has defined a separate and discreet process for finding the root cause of incidents and removing them from the infrastructure. This is Problem Management – a highly technical, behind-the-front-lines process with quality as the primary metric. Many traditional IT practitioners (and MSPs) mentally include the goals of this process in Incident Management. While this is understandable, it is sometimes counterproductive. In a well-meaning attempt to fix a problem once and for all, the technical professionals may negatively impact the availability of an IT service.

It is therefore essential for the MSP staff to understand the difference between an incident and a problem to allow them to determine the proper course of action for each situation. In practice, an MSP will find the most important element of Problem Management to be well defined, shared goals with the customer.

Change Management

The single most important process for an MSP to master early on is Change Management – the single control point for when, where and how a change is promoted to the production environment. This is the ITIL process that will receive the most scrutiny by a SOX auditor. Today, without question, most incidents are caused by IT. When changes are implemented in the production environment, frequent results include outages, lack of availability and breaches in service level. For maximum effectiveness, there should be a single Change Management process across the enterprise.

If an MSP has responsibility for the entire infrastructure, then they can define and dictate a detailed Change Management process for all parties to follow; however, more often the MSP is responsible for changing 'parts' of the infrastructure and contractually responsible for the availability of those 'parts'. This is where a mature, highly integrated Change Management process between the customer and the MSP is essential. If the process is not integrated, two (or more) change processes will be in use, causing unnecessary friction between the two organizations. For example, the MSP may not rush a change because of the risk; but, if the customer wants it, or the customer makes a change that impacts the MSP's service levels, whose fault is it?

The recommendation is to determine which change process better suits the current requirements of the customer. Two change processes simply do not work. There must be absolute agreement as to the areas of responsibility and a clear delineation of change ownership and implementation responsibilities, schedules and contingencies.

Configuration Management

Most MSPs currently use automated discovery tools to determine the hardware components of an infrastructure. Some tools may even detail the operating system and application software installed. This is the beginning of ITIL's Configuration Management process. Utilizing a Configuration Management Database (CMDB), ITIL defines a logical model of the IT infrastructure, including each component and its relationships with other components. Today, most Configuration Management is fragmented in a dizzying array of spreadsheets, databases, documents and note pads. Ideally, this database should include every hardware and software component in the infrastructure, its accompanying documentation, pertinent agreements and contracts, services and perhaps, people.

The end result is a single place to achieve a complete and accurate view of the infrastructure. Most existing IT organizations do not have a mature Configuration Management process. Out of sheer necessity, most MSPs already have much more mature Configuration Management than their clients. Without question, the MSP will include in their client CMDB all the infrastructure components within their realm of responsibility; but, this could also be an opportunity to further serve the needs of the customer and the MSP. One of the key benefits of mature Configuration Management is more effective assessment of the risks and impacts of changes. MSPs can therefore achieve greater availability and stability of the infrastructure through effective Configuration Management.

Release Management

While Change Management is considered a control process, Release Management is not. Its singular goal is protecting the live environment when a new release launches into production. This is accomplished through the co-ordination and facilitation of project management, application development, Change Management, technical staff, service desk and the customer. Both the customer and MSP will have releases. To manage them effectively, there should be one enterprise wide Release Management process encompassing all parties.

MSPs should embrace this process as a method of improving infrastructure stability, enhancing availability and increasing the velocity of stable changes. Release Management should not be confused with Change Management; rather, it is the full integration of mature Change, Configuration and Release Management that will enable MSPs to achieve the challenging service levels being demanded by today's customers in an efficient and profitable manner.

3.3.2 Service Delivery processes

Service Level Management

Service Level Management (SLM) should be familiar territory for MSPs. Often, an MSP's contract with the customer is elaborated upon with a number of Service Level Agreements (SLAs). At the very heart of the MSP's relationship with its customer is the setting of expectations or service levels and then meeting them.

Often, even in practice, SLAs are negotiated at the beginning of the relationship in the mistaken belief that SLAs *are* SLM. This is not the case. ITIL indicates that SLM begins with gathering Service Level Requirements from the customer. For an MSP, this typically occurs through the Request For Proposal and Due Diligence processes. Next, a Service Catalog is developed to identify the services available from IT. Then, internal Operational Level Agreements (OLAs) are identified and negotiated with other IT departments and external Underpinning Contracts (UCs) are established with third party vendors. Finally, an SLA is negotiated with the customer based on the services detailed in the Service Catalog and the fees the customer is willing to pay. ITIL's SLM approach allows both parties to recognize the customer needs, the provider's capabilities and the subsequent costs involved. It is this clear definition that moves the MSP onto the right path for supporting agreements and SLAs.

Financial Management

Linked closely to SLM is the area of Financial Management. The major process activities in ITIL's definition are budgeting, accounting and charging. SLM is based on a fee-for-service concept. The customer is entitled to the highest level of service they can afford; however, before any IT service provider can charge for services, they must understand their costs. This means not only understanding them annually in broad categories, but also monthly at a level of detail that can generate meaningful reports for the customer.

Ideally, an MSP will be able to negotiate an SLA with a customer from a position of complete and accurate knowledge of their costs, broken down by service, by month, by seat, etc. Subsequent operational reporting should also be available at this level of detail so that both the customer and the MSP can have an accurate view of the current financial situation.

Availability Management

Usually, the availability metrics required by the customer are defined in the SLA. Therefore, ITIL's Availability Management process would assist in managing internal operations for maximum availability. In the case of an MSP, Availability Management becomes the assignment of a single point of accountability for availability – a higher level view of system availability and more importantly, IT service availability.

The goal is to manage availability by looking at each service aspect – business criticality, reliability, maintainability/serviceability, resilience, etc. – from the technical, the customer and the MSP point of view. This process, by definition, requires the use of extensive monitoring tools which are often already in place. If the data is generated by disparate toolsets, that information must be combined to create the 'big picture' of availability.

Capacity Management

Capacity Management is not new to IT. There has always been a requirement to plan ahead and make sure there is enough disk space, bandwidth and processor cycles to accommodate the needs of the business. In the past, IT has been somewhat haphazard in managing capacity, last minute purchases, quick moves, etc. ITIL takes a more structured approach that MSPs would be wise to adopt. Using the same monitoring tools and reports from Availability Management, Capacity Management creates a capacity plan based on previous usage experience and in-depth knowledge of future business plans.

This plan is tracked against the rate of actual capacity usage on a monthly, weekly or daily basis. Necessary actions are taken in order to ensure that there is enough capacity and also to maintain availability. Alerts are issued if necessary; but, Capacity Management is primarily a planning and future-focused process. It also embodies the performance aspects (response time, resolution, swap-out, etc.) of service delivery that will be detailed in the SLA with the customer.

IT Service Continuity Management

IT Service Continuity Management rounds out the Service Delivery processes. An MSP must take both an internal and external view. Internally, they may already have a mature disaster recovery program in place for their own operations and for the infrastructure they offer to clients. In many cases, this is a major element of the products and services offered by an MSP and a key deciding factor in choosing an MSP. Externally, an MSP will need to co-ordinate with the customer's existing business continuity plan (BCP).

The key element of coordination needs to be a clear definition of the critical business activities and processes, and exactly which IT service allows them to function. Then, as a subset of the BCP, the IT Service Continuity Plan is developed and structured to highlight the most important IT service first, the second most important, and so on. This is much more than disaster recovery – it is about continuing the business by continuing IT services.

The ISO 20000 standard combines Availability Management and IT Service Continuity Management. This makes sense because continuity can be viewed as a function of availability. The MSP may be considered as a self-contained atomic unit with appropriate service levels that sit inside the customer's larger business continuity plan. The MSP must also take great care that there is no single point of failure shared by the MSP and the customer.

In conclusion, MSPs must become knowledgeable of and experienced in ITIL processes if they are to provide services to a customer base that is expanding its own ITIL knowledge. It will be the ability of an MSP to integrate its own processes with customers in a seamless way while maintaining ITIL integrity that will define the successful MSP of the future.

3.3.3 MSP Dilemma: Integrated processes mean integrated tools

While each ITIL process is an important and uniquely structured set of activities which can achieve substantial positive results for IT even when applied on a stand-alone basis, it is when real integration is achieved through process maturity that the payback of ITIL significantly increases.

Experience has demonstrated that process integration flourishes in an automated environment. Without true integrated automation and work flow technology, the operational processes bog down under the crush of manual data collection and recording. As a result, efficiencies in time, money and staff evaporate in a cloud of paper-based forms and bureaucratic procedures. In today's environment, nearly every customer has an automated workflow management or ticketing system in place. MSPs often have systems that have been customized for efficient delivery of their services. Typically, the customer's system and the MSP's system are different, or even incompatible. Interfaces can be crafted, but this adds time and money to the process.

Positive developments are emerging on this front from the tool vendors themselves. Nearly every major vendor is focusing their development efforts on ITIL. Recognizing that different tools will always need to integrate, the vendors are creating standard interfaces, or making it easier to import and export data on a batch or real time basis.

Given the reality of ITIL's focus on integration, MSPs often find themselves in a difficult position. MSPs understand that integration is the way to achieve efficiencies that are, in most cases, better than their clients'. MSPs may propose to take over specific related IT areas and integrate them in order to bring these greater efficiencies to the client. But, for the most part, MSPs are not able to select which areas they will be responsible for. They are 'told' which parts of IT the customer wants to outsource. Today, fewer and fewer requests for proposals (RFPs) are issued seeking an MSP for the entire IT operation or data centers. Instead, most RFPs issued focus on a single area of IT such as the Help Desk (HD), the network, shrink-wrap applications support and the like. Since MSPs are in business to be profitable, they bid for and win these targeted contracts. And they are able to pass on efficiencies although not to the degree that a fully integrated approach would provide.

3.3.4 Metrics

All successful contractual relationships are based on both sides meeting common expectations. The MSP/client relationship is no different. The final contract will spell out specific goals and objectives that need to be met, specific indicators that need to be measured, how often and how they will be reported and communicated. All MSPs expect to be measured; but, the 'targeted' or 'modular' approach to outsourcing, which may be the correct solution for the client, can cause disconnect with the measurement of true progress in IT.

One example is the historically-revered metric for HDs of First Call Resolution (FCR): The percentage of calls resolved by the HD before the customer hangs up the first time. Ideally, the FCR is around 80% and should stay high over time; however, this is strictly an operational view of the HD. It assumes that the HD is not integrated with the rest of IT, and therefore has no control or input into the number of incidents generated. Within ITIL, this function is an integrated part of a larger incident reduction strategy. Taking this integrated view, it would seem logical to assume that over time, the FCR would actually *decrease* since IT would become aware of repeat incidents and, through Problem Management, eliminate the root cause and, by extension, the incidents.

Now comes the dilemma for the MSP. MSPs clearly understand the relationship between eliminating recorded incidents and improving the stability of the IT infrastructure. But, they find themselves executing an existing contract for 'just the Help Desk' with a financial incentive to maintain or increase the number of calls (paid per call) and a quality metric of maintaining a high FCR. Under these circumstances, there is no incentive for the MSP to improve IT quality. While the MSP may be 'successful' under the terms of the contract and the customer may even be pleased with the MSP's performance, the higher and more strategic goal of greater infrastructure availability and stability goes wanting.

Viewed through an ITIL lens, there is both good news and bad news here. The good news is that it is probable that once ITIL's common processes, definitions and taxonomy are adopted by both the customer and the MSP, this will simplify and clarify the interfaces and touch points between the MSP and the customer. The bad news is that without true process integration, it will be more difficult to achieve automation of the operational processes due to difficult hand-offs between disparate systems and entities. It will also be difficult to achieve conceptual integration because of a customer's 'targeted' outsourcing approach. The impact of certain metrics may be skewed because of a 'modular' or 'targeted' level of MSP responsibility.

■ 3.4 Summary

As MSPs face increased pressure from potential customers to demonstrate how their services align with ITIL best practices, it is becoming more important for MSPs to adopt the framework. Add to this an ever-increasing legislation minefield, where laws such as SOX are forcing IT organizations and MSPs to ensure they are compliant, and there is another reason to use ITIL. Since ITIL's processes can be harnessed to support a SAS-70 compliance program, it makes sense for MSPs to look to ITIL.

When looking at ITIL and envisioning its use, MSPs should use the following roadmap:

1. MSPs should begin immediately to embrace ITIL and to manage their internal operational processes according to ITIL principles. Only by actively implementing and improving the ITIL processes can an MSP hope to gain ITIL expertise to offer to their customers.
2. MSPs should seek some external acknowledgement of their ITIL achievements (BS15000, ISO20000, independent process assessments, etc.) to publicly demonstrate that their own IT operational processes are in line with the ITIL framework.
3. MSPs should engage their customers in process discussions to enhance the MSP's offerings. MSPs should strive to embed as many of the ITIL processes as possible into their new and renewing contracts.

Moving into the second half of the decade, MSPs have an unprecedented opportunity to capitalize on their already significant process expertise; to lead their customers towards true operational excellence and realize even higher levels of infrastructure availability, stability and reliability. Embracing and operationally implementing the most widely-recognized framework of IT best practices, ITIL is but the first step on that journey.

Furthermore, while customer organizations continue to adopt ITIL and seek ITIL-compatible IT support via the MSP, they should take into consideration how ITIL functions in an MSP and realize how this can impact on the nature of the customer-MSP relationship.

4

Process Implementation

■ 4.1 Objective

The objective of this chapter is to provide a template for developing process implementation plans that will be usable across a wide range of diverse organizations. The guidelines within this document are designed for use as a general roadmap or plan, for any major process development or re-engineering project.

■ 4.2 Program management

Many organizations, that undertake programs to improve their core IT processes and service delivery capabilities, experience the frustration of failure, or, at best minor successes, in the place of their ambitious goals. The failure of many improvement initiatives can be directly attributed to management's lack of understanding, that by implementing horizontal processes within traditional hierarchal IT organizations, they are in reality changing the IT culture and accountability structures.

By mandating that departments have to work as cross-functional teams as well as technology based silos, a variety of fundamental changes need to take place:

- Defined and repeatable processes need to be overlaid across hierarchal silo-based and technology focused organizational structures, effectively creating a matrix organization. (If it is not documented it is not real.)
- New areas of accountability and responsibilities are defined within functional job descriptions.
- Values, beliefs, and corporate cultures need to be changed from unconstructive departmental competition, to customer-focused co-operation.
- IT staff working within complex processes need to be provided with more general business knowledge as well as skills required for specialized technical activities.

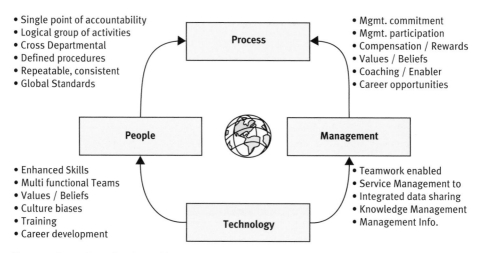

Figure 4.1: Process Re-engineering Model

- To support an integrated process model, collaboration tools must support and automate multi-process data integration and enable workflow automation.
- To embed a new processes orientated and customer focused value system, management must establish new staff performance measures that reward end-to-end service delivery and provide compensation based on process throughput as well as departmental efficiencies.
- New contracts must be put in place with existing suppliers, to clarify new expectations for performance, based on the new values surrounding process adherence, customer-based measures of service delivery expectations.

Implementing ITSM is much, much more than putting pen to paper.

4.3 Process implementation projects

As part the consulting engagement model, Pink Elephant follows a standardized and scalable approach for implementing ITIL processes. This model begins with the creation of a core process design team and the identification of a larger group of stakeholders involved in review, feedback and sign-off activities. A typical project plan includes staged milestones and project activities, which consider the requirements and dependence of process, people, and technology.

The process implementation model has been designed to facilitate a greater level of success for project completion and process embedding. The high-level project model demonstrates the integration and sequence of activities for a typical process implementation project.

■ 4.4 Process, People and Technology: The Integrated Project Plan

To ensure a greater level of success for project completion and process embedding, organizations need to take a holistic view of process implementation projects. Serious consideration needs to be given to the development and mapping of the three basic elements of any quality improvement initiative: process, people and technology. To concentrate on one area to the detriment of the other can jeopardize the success of the project. The following model demonstrates the integration and sequence of activities for a typical process implementation project.

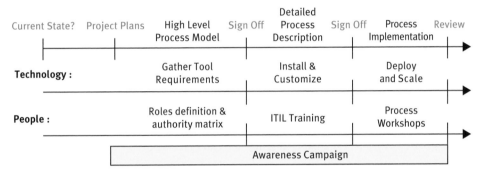

Figure 4.2: Integrated Process Implementation Model

Process implementation is a complex, integrated and multi faceted set of activities, and as such warrants the use of a formal project methodology such as PRINCE2. The recommended formal role established to manage process implementation programs is discussed under 'Process Roles And Responsibilities.'

The implementation of each ITIL process follows the model depicted in Figure 4.2. The scope of this chapter covers the development of IT Service Management processes.

4.4.1 Project timelines

A typical project in a single location will take between four and six months to complete based on the model illustrated in Figure 4.2. The reason for this duration is related to several factors:

1. Internal resources are typically assigned to the project in a part-time capacity with at best, two to three days a week being made available for status and design meetings, as well as the creation of deliverables.
2. With the understanding that process implementation is fundamentally about organizational change, it is necessary to build activities into the project timelines that are focused on receiving feedback and sign-off from process stakeholders. Actual design and creation of deliverables constitutes approximately a third of the time required to implement a re-engineered process. Most organizations that choose to discount consensus building will find that processes designed without the involvement from stakeholders will be highly resisted and most likely fail.
3. Due to the complexities of running a process implementation initiative with strong cross-departmental or regional participation, it is necessary to staff the core process team with diverse members from all stakeholder groups. The added expense and time involved in travel and logistics around these projects requires a creative use of physical as well as virtual participation in relation to design and feedback activities. Co-ordinating the logistics and tools required to facilitate the involvement can add several months to the duration of the project overall. Typically a core team will be brought together more frequently at the beginning of a project, and can then work in a more virtual mode as the project progresses.

In order to meet these time lines the following assumptions have been made:

- executive sponsorship and Process Owners are allocated
- an approved budget is available for internal and external resources over the twelve month period
- funds are available for tool selection and customization according to the ITIL processes being designed and implemented
- there is a political will to define new ongoing roles for process management and co-ordination
- small core teams can be constructed from internal resources
- core team members can be dedicated to their perspective projects at a minimum of three days per week

Expected Project Deliverables:

- documented and formalized process and procedures
- documented and formalized process policies
- automation requirements defined and customized, within technology availability and constraints
- documented and defined awareness campaign and training activities for process implementation
- documented and formalized management reports and key performance indicators
- documented and formalized ongoing roles and responsibilities for the management and continued ownership and improvement of the process

■ 4.5 Implementation Roles

Typical roles required for a process implementation program:

4.5.1 Process Owner

The initial planning phase of an ITIL program must include the establishment of the role of Process Owner. This key role is accountable for the overall quality of the process and oversees the management of, and organizational compliance to the process flows, procedures, models, policies and technologies associated with the IT business process.

The Process Owner performs the essential role of process champion, design lead, advocate, and coach. Typically, a Process Owner should be a senior level manager with credibility, influence and authority across the various areas impacted by the activities of the process. The Process Owner is required to have the ability to influence and assure compliance to the policies and procedures put in place across the cultural and departmental silos of the IT organization.

A Process Owner's job is not necessarily to do the hands on process re-engineering but to ensure that it gets done. They typically assemble the project team, obtain the resources that the team requires, protect the team from internal politics and work to gain co-operation from the other executives and managers whose functional groups are involved in the process. This role's responsibilities do not end with the successful embedding of a new process. In a process-oriented company, the Process Owner remains responsible for the integrity, communication, functionality, performance, compliance and business relevance of the process.

For global projects it is critical to implement a tiered governance and Process Ownership model that provides the flexibility and necessary structure to maintain process consistency across the various regions.

4.5.2 Core process team

Each core process team would consist of between four and six members, who will include the Process Owner in addition to cross-functional representatives from key departments, functional groups and regions within the organization. The make-up and composition of this team is a critical success factor in the overall success of the design, acceptance and effective implementation of the processes. In a global initiative, a regional representative will typically assume the role of process manager or regional Process Owner and be responsible for further co-ordinating and defining the process procedures, tool customizations and implementation strategies required to deploy the process in their specific region. The core process team members should expect to spend at least two to three days a week on the design and deliverable creation activities defined in the projects.

The majority of the actual work of process development and re-engineering is the job of the core process team. They will develop the high-level process model based on the ITIL framework and based on template examples or internal organizational documents.

4.5.3 Stakeholder groups and subject matter experts

In order to maintain a control on cost but yet handle the cross-functional requirements for feedback, expertise, and sign off, additional stakeholder and subject matter experts will be defined and brought into the project at key times. The project work assigned to these individuals should not require significant changes in the volume of daily activities and workload, but will add time to the duration of the project. It is important to re-iterate that the inclusion of these roles and activities in the project is critical for addressing political constraints and for ensuring the long-term success of the process initiative.

4.5.4 Internal and external process advisors

Process Owners, project managers and the core process teams focus is on the specific re-engineering activities being carried out in the organization. The process advisor role is to provide strategic, tactical and operational knowledge transfer at the right place, at the right time and in the right quantity, in order to facilitate the activities of the entire project. The process advisor has the responsibility of enabling and supporting the Process Owners, project manager and the process teams with the correct knowledge, methods and tools.

The process advisor also brings to the project the experience of past implementations and is equipped with in-depth knowledge of best practice, time saving strategies and templates. This role does not have to be dedicated to the project 100%. Typically, the process advisor expends the majority of their efforts at the start of the project conducting training and awareness seminars to ensure the project begins well and is equipped with the knowledge required. From that point forward the process advisor interacts with the project at key milestones.

The process improvement program will be greatly assisted by the correct and timely use of both internal and external advisors.

■ 4.6 Consulting Roles

Pink Elephant provides several defined roles and resources for implementation projects. These roles have been designed to provide the right level of experience and advice to the organization and the process design teams. A typical implementation project will have a managing consultant overseeing the overall relationship with the organizational sponsors and Process Owners.

A senior consultant provides subject matter expertise and an advisor role to the Process Owner and process design teams. This role will provide most of the knowledge transfer in the beginning phases of the project and then will work with the team on a periodic and decreasing basis as the project matures in its lifecycle.

In addition, Pink Elephant can provide hands on assistance with deliverables alongside the process team members. This role is typically handled by a Pink Elephant process consultant and can be shared between multiple process projects.

Table 4.1 provides a visual representation of the model used in standard engagement activities:

Service Delivery	Project Role	Organizational Position
Executive Sponsor Managing Consultant	**Executive Sponsor** *Strategic Vision and Direction*	CIO and Executive
	Process Sponsor *Tactical Integration and Change*	Director Senior Manager
Managing Consultant Senior Consultant	**Process Owner** *Process Design and Training*	Director Senior Manager
	Project Manager *Template Schedules*	Internal PMO
Senior Consultants Consultants	**Team Leads or Process Managers** *Roles and Responsibilities*	Specialists and Operational Staff
	Stakeholder and Subject Matter Experts (SME) *Training and Advisory*	Managers or Specialists
	Process Team Members (Internal and External) *Documentation/Workflow/Policy*	Specialists and Operational Staff

Table 4.1: Project Roles

■ 4.7 High Level Process Model Development

The first phase of the project plan is the development of the high-level process model. The high-level process model is critical to understand the drivers for staffing requirements and tool selection. In its most elemental form, the high level process model maps the key process steps in a sequential flowchart design as shown in Figure 4.3.

As Figure 4.4 illustrates, this high-level process model will map the flow and lifecycle of inputs entering the process, through to the output of desired results. Through the identification of process activities and process integration points, decisions can be made according to staff

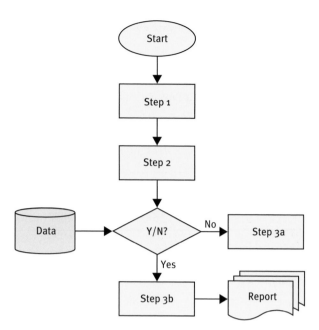

Figure 4.3: Basic High-Level Process Model

roles, skills and competencies. Also, areas for automation will become clear as detail is developed within the activities.

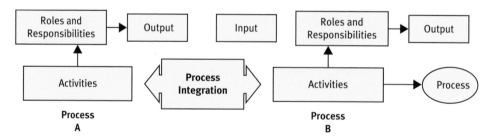

Figure 4.4: High-Level Process Model and Process Integration

The goal of this phase is to establish the basic requirements that will set the tone and the direction of all future work. The high-level process model describes the following components:

1. What is the objective of the process and how does it integrate with other processes?
2. What are the activities of the process and how do they flow from a sequential and parallel perspective?

3. What decision-points exist within the process and what information is required to make the decision?
4. Which are the roles that interact in the process and what do they do?

These points can be summarized into the following statements.

- What is it and what is the point? (ie What is the purpose of the process and its role in the framework?)
- What happens when?
- Who gets to do it?

It is absolutely critical to establish these elements and gain political consensus on these points in the high-level process design phase, before moving the project forward. Ineffective consensus-making at this point, will result in disagreements and excessive debate over basic decision on what, when and who, during the definition of policies, procedures and deployment training.

The primary tools that are presented here are sample flow diagrams representing a deployable process model and description as well as an Authority Matrix which represents a tool to facilitate the mapping of roles to a process flow.

■ 4.8 Detailed design

After the high-level process model has been developed and illustrated in a flow diagram the process needs to be developed down to another level of detail in order to be truly executable.

4.8.1 Process procedures

After the high-level process model has been developed and illustrated in a flow diagram or model, detailed procedures need to be developed to document each activity. Process dependencies will also have to be worked out such as priority indicators, categorization schemes and escalation models.

The development of adequate procedures is the activity that ensures that a process flow is documented with enough detail to allow consistent execution and the clear handling of process exceptions.

In short, procedures should:

- describe clusters of sequential and/or related activities that together realize the process objective
- be started by an external trigger (inputs)

- have connections to other procedures
- describe WHO, WHAT, WHEN and WHERE

Example procedures required for change management:

- define proposal for major change
- handling an RFC
- handling an urgent change
- production of management information

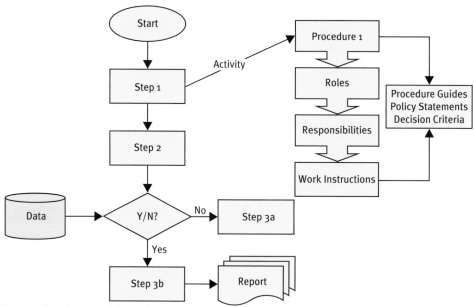

Figure 4.5: Procedures to work instructions

4.8.2 Development of work instructions

A work instruction by definition is a detailed, sequential, step-by-step description of HOW to perform a task in exactly the same way each time. As illustrated in Figure 4.5, work instructions are derived from the high-level process model in an iterative activity that proceeds down through each high-level process step, defining procedures that are comprised of more detailed work instructions (ie descriptive process steps help define WHAT needs done, finally to HOW to do it). Work instructions are generally required for sections of procedures that allow no deviation.

Work instructions:

- describe HOW an activity is performed
- are required in ISO certified organizations

These are necessary for:

- complex activities (eg more than one department involved a the same time)
- activities that need to be performed identical every single time (eg back up)
- inexperienced / unskilled workforce

4.8.3 Policies

Policies have to be defined in order to ensure that all parties use the flow consistently. Without these policy statements and documents the actual use of the flow may be available for interpretation.

Example polices include:

Incident Management

- incident categorization and classification models
- assignment, escalation and notification models
- major incident review policy

Change Management

- request for change lead time policy
- change classification
- change approval requirements

Problem Management

- major incident review

Configuration Management

- CI update frequency
- which attributes require change approval for modification

4.9 Process Roles and Responsibilities

Once detailed procedures and work instructions have been developed, an organization has to design the new staffing model required to support the process and more importantly, the process framework. This often represents a challenge for organizations as it is the critical point where IT leadership stakeholders begin clearly to recognize the extent of required changes to the status quo and the impact this may have on their sphere of influence and reporting structure. The effectiveness of the Sponsorship Communication Strategy and the Program Awareness Campaign will be evident by the degree of (and nature of) resistance experienced at this strategic point in the detailed process design phase.

Clear definition of accountability and responsibility is a critical success factor for any process implementation project. Without this step, functional staff are unclear as to their roles and responsibilities within the new process, and revert back to how the activities were achieved before.

4.9.1 R. A. C. I. Responsibility Model

Once the detailed workflow has been developed, the project team needs to map its organization to process activities. The activities identified in the detailed workflow may include new or changed responsibilities for functional groups. When making these changes managers and employees will ask, 'What is my role?' and 'Who is responsible for what?'

Explicit agreement for cross-functional roles and responsibilities are critical success factors for any project or process. The RACI model, used in project planning (eg PMBOK), quality management (eg Six Sigma), and process design (eg ITIL) is a powerful yet simple tool for assigning and agreeing to cross-functional responsibilities for carrying out process activities. RACI is an acronym for the four roles it defines, Responsible, Accountable, Consulted, and Informed.

The benefits of using the RACI tool to document responsibilities include:

*   helps organizations sort out and clarify responsibilities by assigning future responsibilities and defining how responsibilities will change
*   helps define a matrix organization where accountability and responsibility are distributed across departments, groups, and individuals
*   helps to eliminate ambiguities with respect to responsibilities which could otherwise lead to wasted energy and emotional reactions between groups or individuals
*   helps to deliver the coordination amongst people who need to work together
*   helps improve communication to those who 'need to know' and minimizes the need for redundant communication
*   makes everyone's roles and commitments visible

RACI Role Definitions

Responsible: 'The Doer' - The R is responsible for executing or performing the activity. Responsibility can be shared by multiple roles as long as the conditions where a particular role is responsible are clearly documented and communicated.

Accountable: 'The buck stops here' - The A is the one person who is ultimately responsible for the activity, decision, or process results. This person has yes/no authority. Only one person can be accountable for each activity. Authority must accompany accountability.

Consulted: 'In the loop' - The C is the person or people who are consulted and whose opinion is sought prior to a final decision or action. These people either have a particular expertise they can contribute to specific decisions (ie their advice will be sought) or who must be consulted for some other reason before a final decision is made (eg the person with the authority to approve spending money is often in a consulting role where spend is required). This is a two-way communication with input required from the consulted person or people.

Informed: 'Keep in the picture' - The I is the person or people who are kept up-to-date on progress and/or after a decision or action is taken. These people may be affected by the activity/decision and therefore need to be kept informed, but do not participate in the effort. This is a one-way communication.

4.9.2 Developing the RACI Matrix

The *ITIL Serviced Design* book identifies six steps required to develop, gain agreement, implement, and maintain process roles and responsibilities using the RACI model. Pink Elephant's Process Documentation Guidelines describe *how* to accomplish each of these steps.

Groups and/or Functions

	Process Owner	Process Manager	Process Analyst Role 1	Process Analyst Role 2
Activity 1				
Activity 2				
Activity 3				
Activity 4				

(Left axis label: Activities/Decisions)

Figure 4.6: RACI Matrix Template

4.9.3 Identify the activities

Review the detailed level workflow diagrams and note all of the activity and decision shapes that were designated as needing a procedure or work instruction; noted with a thicker line on the shape border. These are the activities where a person or people are either directly or indirectly involved.

List the activities down the left-hand side of the RACI table using the following guidelines for writing effective titles:
- activity titles should be singular
  - write: 'Record Incident Ticket'
  - do not write: 'Record Incident Tickets'
- Each word in the activity title should begin with a capital letter
  - write: 'Match the Incident Against Existing Incident Records'
  - do not write: 'Match the incident against existing Incident records'
- Activity titles should start with an adverb/verb
  - write: 'Prioritizing a Ticket'
  - do not write: 'The Ticket Should be Prioritized

4.9.4   Identify/define the functional roles

Functional roles include a Process Owner, Process Manager, and any functional group or individual who may be accountable, responsible, consulted, or informed for one or more activity.

Groups and individuals may include people directly involved in the process activities, managers and committees who apply controls to the process activities, and individuals or groups outside the organization who support or have an impact on process activities (eg a hardware vendor).

Functional roles for one ITIL process may be needed in another ITIL process where activities that integrate the processes exist.

List the functional roles across the top of the RACI table starting with the roles having the largest direct involvement first. Additional functional roles may be discovered while walking through the task of 'assigning the RACI codes'.

4.9.5   Conduct meetings and assign the RACI codes

Assigning RACI codes should be done by a small but representative and empowered group. This group is allocating changed or new responsibilities for individuals across the organization. Disagreements between functional managers and individuals with changed responsibilities should be anticipated and planned.

The Process Owner should either conduct the meeting(s) or sponsor an independent facilitator to conduct the meeting so that the Process Owner is free to participate in the discussions.

Working across each row, identify the responsibility (A, R, C, or I) each functional group/individual has with respect to the activity, if any. Place the appropriate letter in the corresponding cell or, if the functional entity has no responsibility, leave the cell blank.

4.9.6 Identify any gaps or overlaps

A process lacking effectiveness and efficiency can often be tracked back to a fault in the RACI matrix. This might be a problem in assigning roles and responsibilities or a problem with the detailed level workflow that is more clearly identified while assigning roles and responsibilities.

An analysis of the completed RACI matrix should be conducted using the following guidelines:

The Importance of the A

The RACI model allocates accountability row by row. This means that even though there can only be one A per row, each row is assessed separately and the A can be allocated differently between rows (or activities). If not carefully planned and managed, accountability for related activities could be allocated to different functional groups or individuals. Doing so will minimize the likelihood that the end-to-end process will be reliably and successfully executed each time.

> For example, within Incident Management, if accountability is allocated to the Service Desk Manager for activities such as recording an incident and initial support, then later in the workflow accountability shifts to an Operations Manager for incidents that have been escalated, a potential for time-delays and incomplete execution of the entire process is created.

Best practice is that, for any set of related activities, one role is accountable for the whole set of activities. The person or people assigned this role must have the authority across the organization to hold the people responsible for executing each of the activities accountable their work.

Regardless of the Accountability allocated on an activity-by-activity basis, the Process Owner is responsible for ensuring that his process is being performed according to the agreed and documented process and is meeting the aims of the process definition. In other words the Process Owner is accountable for overseeing and managing the overall process and making the required judgment calls when conflicts arise. If the Process Owner does not have this higher level end-to-end accountability and authority the organization will end up with sub-optimized effort and weak process results.

RACI guidelines suggest pushing accountability and responsibility, with appropriate authority, down the organization, at the level closest to the action or knowledge, where possible. This is a good practice for day-to-day operational activities. However, realize that the Process Owner has accountability and responsibility to review the process through KPIs and address any issues with the running of the process. The Process Owner has the ultimate accountability.

Testing for Possible Problems
- more than one A - only one role can be accountable for a given activity
- no As - at least one role must be assigned accountability (A) to each activity
- too many Rs in one activity - too many roles responsible often mean that no one takes responsibility. Responsibility may be shared, but only if roles are clear
- no Rs - at least one person must be responsible

- wrong Rs - do the people given the responsibility for executing the activity have the competence, knowledge, and information necessary to complete their role?
- too many Cs - do so many people need to be consulted prior to executing an activity? What are the benefits and can the extra time be justified?
- too many Is - does everyone need to know? In an age of information overload it is best to inform only those people who need to know
- no Cs and Is - are the communication channels open to enable people and departments to talk to each other and keeping each other up-to-date?
- no Spaces - every cell within the matrix need NOT be filled in

4.9.7 Distribute the chart and incorporate feedback

Once the *draft* RACI matrix is complete it needs to be distributed to all of the managers who have staff involved in the new responsibilities. In a perfect situation, agreement and buy-in will be reached amongst these managers for the activities in which their staff has a role. However, there is almost always disagreement. The project team should be prepared to answer questions such as 'What value does that role/person provide?'

In some cases, additional facilitated meetings are needed to help educate the managers about how they and their groups will work together. The final outcome should be consensus and a completed RACI matrix. In some cases the most senior person needs to intercede and make the final decisions. In either case, once the final RACI matrix is complete, all mangers will be required to manage their teams according to the new responsibilities.

4.9.8 Ensure that allocations are being followed (compliance)

The RACI matrix must be published publicly and discussed with all those affected. The communication and reinforcement of the new role definitions are accomplished through meetings and/or training sessions with all departments and individuals directly or indirectly involved. Follow-up must be conducted to ensure that relationships defined in the process are being adhered to and to encourage participants to live the roles.

Going through the exercise of developing a RACI chart will gain meaning only when the outcomes are acted upon. Otherwise, the company will have wasted time on something that winds up being a non-implemented planning tool.

4.9.9 Critical cultural considerations

Culture in an organization is defined as a self-reinforcing set of beliefs, attitudes and behaviors. Culture is one of the most resistant elements of organizational behavior, and is extremely difficult to change. To be successful, process re-engineering projects must consider current culture in order to change these beliefs, attitudes and behaviors effectively. Messages conveyed from senior management in an organization continually re-enforce current culture for the positive or negative. Performance reward systems, stories of company origin and early successes of founders, physical symbols and company icons constantly enforce the message of the current culture. These messages provide people in the organization with unspoken guidelines for the direction of acceptable behavior patterns. People quickly determine what is 'good and bad behavior' or what should be accepted or rejected from the message received from the culture.

Organizational culture influences managerial behavior, which in turn directly influences company plans, policies and organizational direction. In short, culture is shaped and transformed by consistent patterns of management action. This means that re-shaping of culture cannot be achieved in the short term. Cultural changes must be continually reinforced by consistent action over the long-term. A new process, attitude or slogan will not change culture if the underlying reward systems and messages of the current culture are not changed permanently. Quick fixes and spontaneous attempts to change culture will undoubtedly fail without long-term planning, commitment and communication demonstrated by senior management.

■ 4.10 Process implementation considerations

A practical implementation of service management should include:

* 'quick wins' to demonstrate the benefits of service management
* starting with something simple and adopting a phased approach
* involving customers, especially those that have been critical of the service
* explaining the differences that will be seen by customers
* involving third party service suppliers
* explaining what is being done and why to everyone involved or affected; support staff are often cautious about changes; it is particularly important that they understand the benefits to overcome their resistance
* involve staff wherever possible in designing improved process / workflow, facilitate ownership interest, educating staff and managers to become service managers

Implementation times

Throughput times for an implementation project are dependent upon the scale, required customization, and degree of complexity of each organization. In some organizations several processes can be implemented concurrently, subject to the following considerations:

* size of the overall IT operation
* scope of the role selected for each process
* degree of integration with other IT processes
* number of processes to be implemented
* quality and number of assigned staff
* speed of management decision-making

4.11 Applicability / Scalability

The size of the organization is an important factor when implementing ITIL processes (or indeed for any other kind of change). In a small organization, many of the roles defined may well be the responsibility of one person.

Although in practice, a large number of factors in the organization will have an impact on which combinations work best, based on best practices, the following can be said on role sharing:

- There is a tension between Incident and Problem Management, because of their conflicting goals. The incident manager is responsible for quickly minimizing the effect of incidents for users. The problem manager's task is to find the underlying problem and is less interested in the continuity of the users' activities. When combining these two roles, this tension should be acknowledged.
- There is a similar tension between Problem and Change Management. When combining these roles, there is the danger of changes quickly being implemented by the problem manager, who is the same person. No checks and balances exist.
- Roles that are quite commonly shared are those of configuration manager and release manager. Both tasks have an administrative component and are concerned with maintaining an up to date database.
- Configuration and Change Management can easily be shared as the configuration manager uses CMDB information and there is no direct conflict of interest.

4.12 Critical Success Factors

There are several factors that will need to be considered to ensure a greater degree of project success:

Business decisions
Decisions on the implementation of a process should be guided by the organization's predefined process maturity goals.

Time for planning and review
Enough time should be given to the careful consideration of project plans, process goals and tool requirements to ensure qualified decisions are made in respect of process implementation.

Mutual terms of reference
When dealing with multiple business units or complex organizations, common frames of reference will need to be negotiated and agreed upon such as categorization, priority (impact and urgency indicators) and escalation models. These values will have to be developed before a shared tool can be fully configured and used.

Knowledge of the people
The Process Owners and operators, who will work at developing a common sense of purpose for the Service Management process framework, should have hands-on ownership in the

development of this solution. All stakeholders should have a solid understanding of the specific process in which they hold responsibilities as well as an understanding of process integration points within the framework.

Product configuration

Time should be dedicated up front to the proper configuration of the Service Management process automation tool's workflow and values. Detailed procedures and work instructions will have to be documented, based on pre-defined process models, in order to ensure efficient mapping of process to technology.

Central focus on control and integration

Maturity within the ITIL Service Management framework focuses on the integration of processes. Insure that inputs and outputs to each process are defined and automated where possible.

To limit the degree of rework in phased process implementation projects, Process Owners and key stakeholders should develop the integrated framework model early in the initial process design and implementation planning activities, and use it as the high-level architectural blueprint for all subsequent process implementations.

Project review

After the implementation of an ITIL process, a formal review should be done by the organization.

Organizational culture and management commitment

This is the cornerstone of all success factors. Without demonstrated commitment and direct participation from senior management, a process initiative or cultural change is severely constrained and most likely will fail.

4.13 Process Embedding Strategy

When it is time to embed a process within an organization, the sequence and timing of activities plays an important role in insuring the success and acceptance of the new processes, procedures and policies.

The critical inputs for this stage of the project are as follows:

- high level process flow
- detailed procedures and work instructions
- guidelines/support and policy documents
- correctly installed and configured tool
- the right skill level and knowledge of staff
- management commitment
- supporting staff commitment to authority matrix
- customer awareness and acceptance

A constraint or limitation on any of the above points could indicate a potential problem with the embedding phase of the project.

■ 4.14 Process workshops / training

This phase in process embedding uses the output from the high level modeling and detailed design phase, and involves user guides, procedure guides, policy documents and other training materials to communicate the new 'way we work'. The goal of this activity is to insure that roles and responsibilities are clearly understood, procedures followed and policy adherence is observed as the IT organization moves forward in a Service Management centered and process based work culture.

4.14.1 Develop lesson plans

Define target groups, for example:

- Service Desk
- team leads
- management
- second and third level support

- set objectives
- develop time frames
- develop workshop / training
- develop specialized presentations
- develop handouts and documentation
- develop marketing material

4.14.2 Schedule workshop and process embedding date

Timing is key when scheduling the workshops. Ideally, the training should be delivered just prior to going live with the new procedures. The timeline in Figure 4.7 illustrates this concept. It is always a best practice to go live in a limited pilot location to minimize any potential impact to the organization.

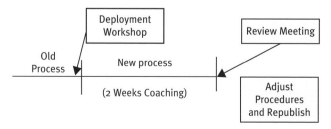

Figure 4.7: Training timeline

4.14.3 Coaching period

After the process start-date, coaching workshops should be offered to prepare the staff to use the new procedures. This coaching serves several important purposes. First, the coaching will function in a quality audit capacity to ensure that the new process and procedures are being adhered to. Second, during this period process functionality will be examined to provide information for the first review. In the case of a pilot project, improvement adjustments can be made for the full implementation of the new process before organization wide application.

4.14.4 Initial process review and adjustment

Following the two weeks of process coaching and monitoring, an initial review should be held on the functionality of the new process. If bottlenecks or improvement actions can be identified, the process and procedures should be modified and republished.

4.15 Detailed activities: Project checklist

- process design and implementation plan
- terms of reference and statement of requirement
- feasibility study
- project brief (high level project definition)
- project initiation document (PID) – a detailed description of work break down and product break down
- appoint a Process Owner
- define a mission statement
- set objectives
- agree on scope, roles and responsibilities
- review experiences, tools and processes at similar sites
- risk analysis
- product selection and overall design
- mount awareness campaign
- recruit and train staff
- development and validation
- pilot project
- pilot review
- implementation
- post implementation review (PIR)
- on-going management and operation
- efficiency and effectiveness reviews
- audit

4.15.1 People involved

- customers and IT staff
- appointment of Process Owners
- support staff
- suppliers, contractors and vendors
- consultants
- project teams
- auditors

4.15.2 Awareness campaign

- sponsorship communication plan
- newsletters
- workshops
- bulletins
- seminars
- presentations
- marketing information
- external education

4.15.3 Systems implementation activities

- acquire and install equipment
- customize tools
- test system
- create hardware and software inventories
- prepare documentation
- train staff
- carry out acceptance testing
- post implementation review and audit

4.15.4 Support tools

- automated wherever possible
- integrated with other SM processes
- provide accurate and timely information

4.15.5 Post-implementation and audit

- reconcile requirements with reality – on time, on budget, deliverables met
- compare activity levels with forecasts
- assess human element
- review effectiveness and efficiency

- identify benefits gained
- reconcile actual and planned roles
- review overall project – how well did it go?
- prepare review reports
- quality management (assurance and control)

4.16 Communication plan

Communication is a vital component of these culture change dependent projects. A Service Management project will involve many people directly, but typically, the outcome will affect the working lives of many more. Implementing or improving Service Management within an organization requires a cultural change not only by IT employees, but also by IT customers and users as well. Communication around this transformation is essential to its success. It is necessary to ensure that all parties are aware of what is going on and can play a relevant part in the project. For this reason, clarification and planning how the project will communicate with all interested parties is necessary.

A formal communication plan has a direct contribution to the success of the project.

Communication is more than a one-way information stream. It requires continuous attention to the signals (positive and negative) of the various parties involved. Managing communications effectively involves the following steps:

1. formulate vision for change and role of communication
2. analyze current communication structure and culture
3. identify target groups
4. decide for each target group the communication objectives
5. decide for each target group the communication strategy
6. decide for each target group best communication methods and techniques
7. write communication plan
8. realize communication methods and techniques, and communicate
9. measure and evaluate the effect and adjust

A communication plan describes how target groups, contents and media are connected in the timeline of the process implementation project. Much like a project plan, a communication plan will show plans including actions, people, method and budget.

4.17 Evaluation of the project

As the project draws to a close, it is important to analyze how the project was managed and to identify lessons learned. This information can then be used to benefit the project team as well as the organization as a whole. An end project report will typically cover:

- achievement of the project's objectives
- performance against plan (estimated time and costs versus actual)
- effect on the original plan and business case over the time of the project
- statistics on issues raised and changes made
- total impact of changes approved
- statistics on the quality of the work carried out (in relation to stated expectations)
- lessons learned with recommendations
- post project review plan

■ 4.18 Post project review

A business case will have been built based on the premise that the project outcome will deliver benefits to the business over a period of time. The delivery of these stated benefits needs to be assessed at a point after the project has been completed and the process has been in operation. The post project review is used to assess whether the expected benefits have been realized, as well as to investigate if problems have arisen from use of the process.

Each of the benefits mentioned in the business case should be assessed to see how well, if at all, it has been achieved. The post project review should also consider any additional benefits achieved or unexpected problems that arose; both of which can be used to improve future business cases. If necessary follow-up actions may be developed as adjustments or improvement actions are identified.

■ 4.19 Auditing using quality parameters

Process quality parameters can be seen as the 'operational thermometer' of the IT organization. Using quality parameters allows you to determine whether processes are effective and efficient.

There are two types of quality parameters, process specific and generic.

Generic quality parameters for IT Service Management

The following parameters are in fact measurement categories that need to be quantified before a valid assessment can be done. This task will be easier once you have determined the required service levels and internal service requirements. Generic quality parameters to consider include:

- customer satisfaction
- staff satisfaction
- efficiency
- effectiveness

Process specific quality parameters for IT Service Management

Process specific quality parameters are measures of the degree to which the process delivered the desired outcome. Efficiency of key process activities, reliability of process integration points and specific measure of process automation tool efficiency are examples of process specific quality parameters.

The appropriate information will need to be collected to quantify the quality of each parameter. The nature of the information required will vary depending on how an organization decides to measure each aspect. These indicators should be clearly defined at the start of the project so that such benefits can be assessed objectively at a post project review.

■ 4.20 Summary

In conclusion, the purpose of this chapter is to provide a template for developing process implementation plans that will be usable across a wide range of diverse organizations. Managing change and ensuring overall project success is greatly facilitated by the development of a detailed implementation strategy. The guidelines developed within this document are designed for use as a framework or general methodology to consider when undertaking any major process development or re-engineering project. The applicability and level of detail used from this report will depend on the scale and complexity of the project or organization being considered.

In general however, it can be said that process implementation projects vary somewhat from traditional IT projects. They are by nature, culture change dependent projects. Proactive measures to address change resistance, proactive project sponsorship activities and creative communication planning activities must be incorporated into project planning at the earliest phases. Process implementation projects present special challenges for IT organizations, but adequate planning will help ensure an effective implementation strategy.

5

Defining, Modeling and Costing IT Services

5.1 Introduction

In our cost driven economy, IT is facing increasing pressure to account for and reduce cost wherever possible. The old axiom 'you must do more with less' has never had such an impact on IT operations and support as it does today. Thousands of IT managers are being placed in a situation which forces them to defend their staffing levels against both internal as well as external threats. To address this situation, IT executives are being forced to understand better the services they are providing and to provide an accurate cost benefit analysis of why the services they offer are a better value than the services being offered by external groups who, at the very least, offer the promise of fixed or at least known costs.

Of course, the basic requirement to do this is to have a clear definition of what services the IT organization provides, the components and resources that make up the service and what are the associated costs for these services. Understanding the scope, characteristics and costs of defined services allows for better management of the IT infrastructure as a whole. The sad fact of the matter is that very few IT organizations can articulate what they do at this level of detail. Part of the reason for this lack of information is due to the relative process maturity and integration being practiced within many IT organizations.

This chapter examines the fundamental steps for:

- defining IT services
- modeling IT services in a CMDB
- developing service-based IT costing models

These activities are part of three IT processes (Service Level, Configuration and Financial Management for IT) as documented within ITIL®. While other processes have a relationship to this topic, these processes contain activities which directly relate to the problem statement above.

■ 5.2 Defining IT services

It is often said that in order to improve 'something' one must first define it. This is no less true when dealing with the collection of activities that IT organizations execute for their business customers. Typically, when looking at an IT organizational chart one can see a rudimentary breakdown of IT services defined at the directorate or senior management level. Common names for these structures fall under the categories of:

- application development
- operations
- facilitates management (FM)
- IT support
- hosting
- security
- service delivery
- IT or architectural planning

These structures begin to allude to the 'professional' IT services which are being delivered to the customer and provide a starting point for how a certain category of services can be defined that are understood by both the business and the IT organization. While these structural names facilitate the definition of IT services, they also promote a commonly held belief that IT services are silo or departmental-based, when this is not always the case. Much like a process, an IT service typically crosses organizational and functional boundaries.

A major component of Service Level Management is the definition of IT services within a Service Catalog from which Service Level Agreements (SLAs) are negotiated with the client.

The following diagram illustrates how Service Level Management defines IT services, publishes them in a comprehensive Service Catalog and then develops SLAs based on these definitions with its customers.

The first step in the creation of an IT Service Catalog is the definition and development of a comprehensive list of IT services and systems that the IT organization provides to its customer base. In order to accomplish this task it is important to understand some basic rules around naming IT Services.

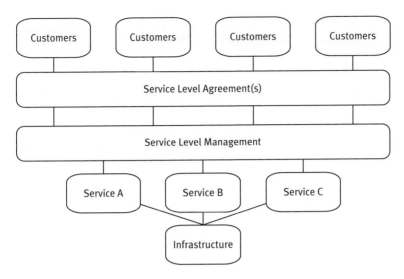

Figure 5.1: Service Level Management

Naming IT Services

> **'What's in a name? That which we call a rose by any other word would smell as sweet.'**
> **Romeo and Juliet (II, ii, 1-2)**

While this approach may work for creative literature it does not work at all when adopting a standard approach for to defining IT Services. While there is room for the creative mind, the structure and naming convention around IT Services should follow basic rules.

First of all, a key benefit of the ITIL library is that it provides a neutral (non partisan) common vocabulary for IT Service Management. If you put 10 IT professionals in a room and ask them what a service is and you will get at least 12 answers.

So to revisit the definition of a Service from Chapter One here are the standard definitions:

IT Service:

One or more technical or professional IT capabilities which enable a business process. Or from an ITIL version 3 perspective: 'A service is a means of delivering value to customers by facilitating outcomes customers want to achieve without the ownership of specific costs and risks.'

An IT Service exhibits the following characteristics:

- fulfills one or more needs of the customer
- supports the customer's business objectives
- is perceived by the customer as a coherent whole or consumable product

Note: By this definition a service is a capability, not a technology solution or vertical domain such as a server environment or a business application.

Perhaps the easiest way to understand what is a service is to consider the Application Service Provider (ASP model). In this model a business unit contracts for the capability of Client Relationship Management (CRM). The ASP manages all of the technical aspects of delivering this application service with the business customer only caring about the outcome of being able to enable and automate their CRM processes.

IT System:

An integrated composite that consists of one or more of the processes, hardware, software, facilities and people, that provides a capability to satisfy a stated need or objective.

An IT System:

- is a collection of resources and configuration items or assets that are necessary to deliver an IT Service
- is sometimes referred to as a Technology Solution

Note: The technology system is the complete composite of IT components from various domains which, when brought together in a relationship, represent a value-added technology solution: for example, a Local Area Network or an application system such as an Enterprise Resource Planning solution. A system is not referring to the application as a stand-alone element, but to all of the components which build the complete solution (application, databases, servers and middleware, etc.).

Configuration Item (CI):

A CI is a component of an IT infrastructure that is part of an IT System.

CIs may vary widely in complexity size and type – from a document or policy to an entire system or a single module or a minor hardware component.

Rules: Based on these two definitions here are some key rules to bear in mind when developing a Service / System structure:

1. A service always refers to a capability or outcome and not a specific technology.
2. A service does not make reference to an organizational function, department or structure. In other words it is organizationally agnostic.
3. A service is supported by one or many systems, eg Messaging is supported by Backberry and Exchange.
4. There are three types of IT services (Business Application Services, Infrastructure Services and Professional Services).

5. Any of the three types of services can either be customer facing or component/supporting services.

6. The moment you start publishing logical and sensible IT Services, expect someone to ask you to tell them how much they cost.

Why the insistence on the first two rules?

Consider that while an IT Service like email is relatively constant; both its underlying technology system and the organization which delivers it are both transient.

A few years ago you may have used CCmail and now your organization leverages Lotus Notes or Microsoft Exchange. Who knows what you will be using in the future. The point is that the service is constant and the technology changes.

Likewise, today you may manage Exchange internally, but tomorrow you may use an ASP model or you might choose to outsource it completely. The point is that a service is constant but who delivers it will change.

Note: For a full description of defining IT Services refer to Chapter One of this book.

■ 5.3 Service Classifications

Along with Service Type, it is also necessary to understand that services should be separated according to three basic classifications. These classifications are especially important when they are to be applied to a costing model. It is important to understand that the list of services distinguished under these classifications must be determined by each organization and will change according to the environment or business model being employed.

5.3.1 Core or essential services:

A core service is a service which is required by all business stakeholders and for which each line of business stakeholder must pay an appropriate share. These services are like 'air', you need them to exist and there is no option to opt out of their use or consumption. Typical examples of Core Services are:

- data \ LAN
- email
- IT support
- voice
- security

5.3.2 Subscription services:

A subscription service is a service that can be chosen in an 'a la carte' manner based on the business function that the customer is engaged in. These services will only appear on the client bill of those clients who specifically use or subscribe to them. Examples of Subscription Services are typically application based services, and are described according to the business process or function they support.

- enterprise resource planning (ERP) services
- power generation systems
- online banking
- trading applications
- HR management
- market research
- enhanced desktop management or forward deployed support

5.3.3 Discretionary/Transactional services:

Discretionary services are services that IT provides on a 'pay-as-you-go' basis. These services are typically only charged back to a client if the client requests them for a special activity outside a standard service package. Examples of discretionary services are:

- project management
- IT Consulting
- architectural reviews of new technology
- procurement services

The full description and detailing of these services in an IT Service Catalog around various options of level and availability is the domain of Service Level Management and is outside the scope of this chapter. For the purposes of modeling and costing, it is enough that services have been defined and classified as a design input for Configuration Management and IT finance. Going forward it is critical that the service definitions used in costing and billing are kept in alignment with the Service Catalog.

■ 5.4 Steps for defining IT services

The following section defines the logical and sequential steps to define a list of IT services. Those steps are:

1. define major business processes
2. define enabling IT services
3. map IT systems To IT services

4. map IT components to IT systems (this step is done by ITIL Configuration Management)

5.4.1 Step 1: Define the business processes

The most appropriate way to define IT services is from a business or customer perspective. To determine this IT must understand how it facilitates the business in enabling the various business processes. Logically it follows that the place to start this activity is to define what the business processes are. The following model is taken from the ITIL book, *Understanding and Improving – The Business Perspective On Your IT Infrastructure*. This model breaks the business processes down into four major categories:

1. management processes
2. support processes
3. innovation processes
4. primary business processes

Each of these categories in turn has sub-processes that need to be defined in order to get down to a useable level of detail to start the service definition activity.

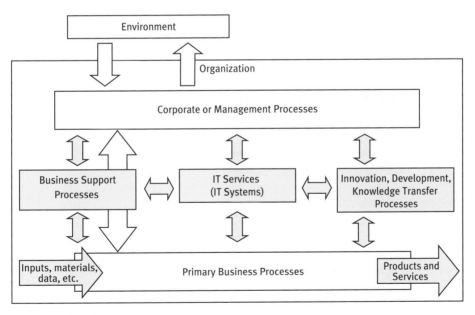

Figure 5.2: Business Processes

5.4.2 Step 2: Defining IT services

Many of the IT services will be defined and named after the business process or function the IT service facilitates. A benefit of aligning the IT service names with business processes is that it improves understanding for both the customer and IT staff on how technology is aligned to meet business objectives.

To illustrate this activity the 'Business Support Processes' category has been highlighted below:

Example Business Support Sub Processes:

examples of typical business processes in this category are:

- HR
- corporate finance
- office support
- logistics and facilities management
- communications

While many of the service names will be common from company to company, each organization needs to go through this exercise in order to define its personal list of IT services. The activity of doing this is a learning step that helps promote a better understanding of true business and IT alignment.

5.4.3   Step 3: Map IT systems to IT services

The next step in this process comes more naturally to technical people since it involves defining and naming the IT systems that the IT organization delivers and supports, and mapping them to the IT service definitions. Remember that an IT system is a collection of components required to deliver a technology solution to a customer. Often, the IT system inherits the name of the primary application that it is delivering. Another principle to keep in mind is that while there is a single IT service definition, there are no limits to how many IT systems can be mapped to this capability.

Some examples of service / systems mappings are:

IT Service	IT System
email	MS Exchange
	Lotus Notes
Shared Infrastructure	Data / LAN
	Voice
	Storage Management
HR Management	PeopleSoft
	Payroll

Table 5.1: Service/system mappings

When all IT services and systems have been defined by Service Level Management, this information is provided to Configuration Management to facilitate the design of the CMDB object model and to financial management for the development of the service-based costing and billing models.

5.4.4 Step 4: Map IT components to IT systems

The final step in this process is the mapping of IT components or CIs to IT systems. This is the function of the ITIL Configuration Management process and will be modeled in the CMDB. The next section of this chapter will cover this in more detail.

5.5 Modeling IT services

Once IT services have been defined and documented the next step is to leverage the Configuration Management process in order to model those services within the CMDB. Through object and data modeling techniques a database of Configuration Items (CIs) can be created to present both a business service view as well as a technology view of how CIs are related, in order to support business processes. In effect, the ultimate goal of Configuration Management is to facilitate the creation of a real-time virtual model of the IT infrastructure in relation to how it supports and delivers IT services.

5.6 Configuration Management Objective

Configuration Management provides a logical model of the infrastructure or a service by identifying, controlling, maintaining and verifying the versions of CIs in existence.

The goals of Configuration Management are to:

- account for all the IT assets and configurations within the organization and its services
- provide accurate information on configurations and their documentation to support all the other service management processes
- provide a sound basis for Incident Management, Problem Management, Change Management and Release Management
- verify the configuration records against the infrastructure and correct any exceptions

Configuration Management is an important part of the ITIL service management framework. It serves as the central hub for information sharing and collaboration.

An asset, in ITIL terminology, is called a Configuration Item (CI). A CI can refer to any type of items the organization wishes to control.

The CMDB must be capable of registering these basic components:

- physical CIs: server, switch, application, database, documents
- logical CIs: IT services, systems, baseline records
- CI Attributes: CPU speed, serial number, version, author, purchase date
- CI Relationships: parent-child, hosts, installed on, provides data feed

■ 5.7   Configuration Management IT service data modeling

In order to model IT services, an object and data model must be developed in order to illustrate how different CI types are represented, which attributes they have and what relationships connect them. The data model dictates how the IT services are mapped into the CMDB. The practical application of this is the creation of logical CI records that represent IT services and how they breakdown into IT system, subsystem and finally physical components. The concept presented by this approach allows the physical CIs (hardware, software, documents, etc.) to be related up into an IT service chain.

To use an analogy:

If the infrastructure is the puzzle, and the CI the puzzle piece, then the Configuration Management object model design is the picture on the puzzle box.

Just as it is difficult to build a puzzle without the picture, it is difficult to understand how various CI's fit into the infrastructure without the object model.

Some key benefits derived from this model are:

- the understanding of how CIs within the scope of the process relate to IT business services
- how direct and indirect asset costs are related to IT services
- how availability figures relate to individual CIs, groupings of CIs and overall service availability targets
- which CIs facilitate multiple IT services
- prioritization of CIs in relation to business criticality and function

For each of the IT business services and technical IT systems defined by the SLM process there will be a record created in the CMDB within the logical structure. Once this structure is built within the tool, the logical structure will remain relatively static and will not change drastically unless a new service is introduced to the environment.

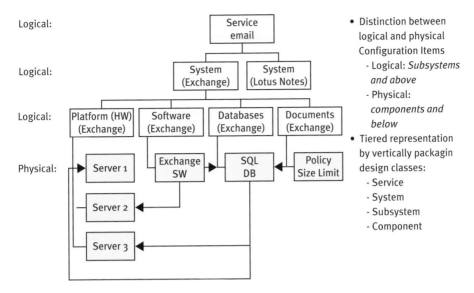

Figure 5.3: Object model and IT services

5.8 Developing a service-based cost model

IT struggles in many areas to become more proactive in the management and delivery of its services to the client. This is nowhere more apparent then in the way that technology costing is typically done.

Regrettably what usually occurs during the year is that all IT costs and expenses are collected into a large cost center or proverbial bucket, which at the end of the fiscal period gets up-ended on the table and then is divided up equally across the clients regardless of use.

There is little to no ability to express accurate costs for providing services to clients, let alone to provide an accurate tracking of how services are consumed by its customers. This practice provides no ability to use costing as a management and planning tool, since you cannot improve what you do not understand.

5.9 Financial management for IT services

Objective: Financial management is the sound stewardship of the monetary resources of the organization. It supports the organization in planning and executing its business objectives and requires consistent application throughout the organization to achieve maximum efficiency and minimum conflict.

An interesting comment that one often hears when speaking to organizations about the discipline of costing is that they are a 'cost center' and as such, they are not in the business of charging for their services. This is often used as a convenient excuse to not look at the disciplines of IT costing in any significant detail. However, the logical response to these organizations is that even though they may not provide a bill to an internal business client, they still have to account for the cost of provisioning IT services to the business, and in turn receive next year's budget allocation. Recently, this has become even more important with the current focus of the market being on cost reduction and financial governance. IT organizations are no longer being afforded the grace they once were, and the business is demanding an accurate accounting and tracking of IT costs related to use and consumption.

Of course, the catch here is that you need to have defined and modeled these services first before you can cost them effectively. Trying to develop a costing methodology without implementing the first two steps outlined in this chapter becomes very difficult if not impossible to do accurately.

5.10 Understanding IT costs

Admittedly, ITIL does not dictate what type of costing methodology should be employed. However, the *ITIL Service Strategy* book does a good job of summarizing Service Economics the two most basic approaches of 'cost-centered accounting' and 'activity or service-based costing'.

At a high level, **cost-centered accounting** is the practice of pointing all costs and expenses in their direct form at a client or organizational entity. This is traditionally the most widely used costing method since it works well with the concept mentioned earlier of allocating the general cost of doing IT across all clients in whatever equitable fashion can be devised.

Activity or service-based costing is the practice of pointing all related costs and expenses at a defined activity or IT service. Once the service has been completely costed, a unit cost is defined. This becomes the tool for understanding how the activity or service can be allocated to a customer based on the consumption of the service.

To further explore these concepts we need to define a few key terms.

Definitions:

Direct costs: clearly attributable to a single customer\service\location
- these costs are directly related and are completely attributable to a specific customer or service

Indirect: shared costs: incurred on behalf of all, or a number of customers\services\ locations
- these costs are shared across a number of customers and services and are allocated according to some driver such as head count or percentage

Unabsorbed or overhead costs: are costs which can not be directly attributed to a customer\ service\location
- these costs are not attributable to a customer or service; examples of overhead costs are executive salaries, general administrative activities

Cost unit: a cost unit is a breakdown of the total cost of a service into a small unit
- a cost unit is a breakdown of an entire service cost into a unit that can be allocated to a consumer; an example of a unit cost is the cost per mailbox for an email service charged to a line of business

It is important to build a costing methodology which includes all three types of cost since a service, which is only costed based on direct costs, will be ultimately under-recovered.

Milk Analogy:
A non-IT example of this principle would be the calculation of the total cost of a glass of milk. You could just account for the cost of the care and feeding of the cows, and your unit cost for the glass of milk might be relatively small. However, when you layer in or allocate a percentage of the farm insurance costs, the mortgage and the lease payments on the farm equipment, the total cost of your glass of milk might double or triple. In essence, everything needs to be paid for eventually.

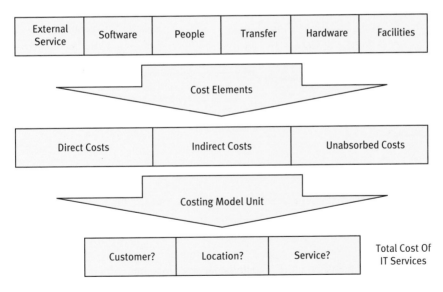

Figure 5.4: IT Costs

While ITIL indicates no preference for either cost-centered accounting or service-based costing, the logical preference would be service, for the simple reason that the philosophy of Service Management is more closely aligned with service-based costing.

5.11 Service-based costing

By its very name, service-based costing suggests an end-to-end view of the costs of delivering an IT service. Practically, this means that a costing methodology and set of cost centers need to be defined using the service definitions provided by the SLM process and as published in the Service Catalog. In principle, this means that the line items appearing on the client bill are synchronized with the services as they are defined within the SLAs, and how CIs are captured and modeled within the CMDB.

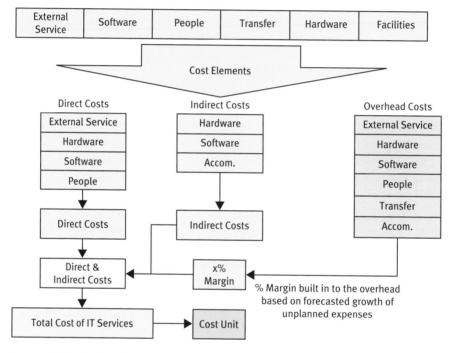

Figure 5.5: Service-based costing

Based on the CIs and roles that are modeled against the IT service in the CMDB, the direct costs for the service can be derived fairly easily through query of the financial attributes recorded against those CIs that have no other service relationship. Also, there will be some CIs which are related to multiple services in a cross-functional capacity. An example would be an application server that hosts multiple applications; the server in question would need to be allocated across however many services it facilitated.

5.12 Component/Supporting services

Another element to consider when establishing the indirect or shared costs is what is referred to as component services. A component service or utility type service is a fully costed service that is not directly displayed on the client bill or cost recovery mechanisms. The result of this decision is that they need to be allocated on top of a direct or client facing service in order to be recovered. Which services are deemed to be component services is a decision of the IT financial process in the development of the costing methodology.

Examples of a component or utility service would be if the IT organization wished to allocate the network service across other services as a shared or indirect cost. A utility type of service might be the cost associated to a data center, mainframe or raised floor facility. These services are allocated against others which are client facing based on some defined driver. A driver is the allocation method used to apportion the costs against other services and might be as simple as a straight percentage, head count, floor space, or number of components.

■ 5.13 Service-based costing steps

The high level steps for costing the services defined by Service Level Management are as follows:

Step 1: define IT services and systems
Step 2: decide on the service classification (core, subscription, discretionary)
Step 3: model the services and systems in the CMDB
Step 4: decide which services and systems will appear directly on the client bill
Step 5: allocate services that are not on the client bill against other services
Step 6: define drivers and an allocation methodology for the component services
Step 7: define a unit cost for the client facing service-based on usage

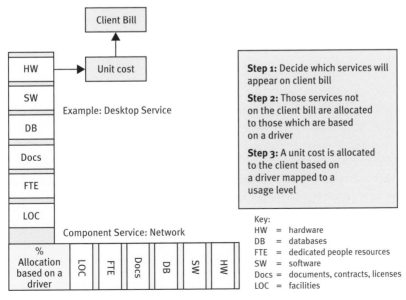

Figure 5.6: Service-based costing – steps

Note: Figure 5.6 illustrates two fully costed services where one is presented on the customer bill (desktop) and the other is allocated as a component service (network) with a percentage of the overall cost of being applied to the total cost of the desktop service.

■ 5.14 Summary

In conclusion, IT organizations are no longer being afforded the grace they once were, and the business is demanding an accurate accounting and tracking of IT costs related to use and consumption. Services need to be defined and managed in a proactive manner that facilitates management decision-making. It is important to understand the integration of Service Level, Configuration and Financial Management and the strength of the integrated model. One could go further to discuss the correlation to Availability, Capacity and IT Service Continuity which should also be synchronized in their development and reporting with the service definitions. Regardless of where your organization is in the pursuit of its Service Management goals, the important thing to keep in mind is that the true power of the ITIL framework is not in the description of best practices for a single process, but in the integration of the overall framework.

6

The Federated CMDB

The emerging capability of federating data sources is the biggest boon and the largest potential pitfall that has arisen for the discipline and process that ITIL calls Configuration Management.

On the surface this may appear to be a contradictory statement. However, as is the case with all good intentions, it all comes down to the application. First and foremost, database federation is an absolute must for a successful CMDB implementation.

6.1 Three applications of CMDB federation

One, and perhaps the most fundamental definition of a federated CMDB is that of a master database (aka the CMDB) that references an external database for a subset of information. Simply put, when we are looking at a record representing a Configuration Item (CI) some of the information we find in the record is stored in the central CMDB and some of the information is stored in an external source or database. The key is to make this appear completely transparent to the person accessing and reviewing the central CMDB record

While federation is important, the challenge we face is that there are three different uses or applications of the term. Of these three uses, two of them represent strategies for data consolidation that are likely roads to long term failure.

The three applications of the term 'federation' are:

1) **CMDB federation is the exception, not the rule.**
   The CMDB is a tool used by all IT Management functions and processes and the effort is made to consolidate and centralize most, if not all, the 'like' data sources into the CMDB. We will link to other data sources only where it makes sense.

2) CMDB federation is the rule, not the exception.

The CMDB is a tool used only for Service Management and there is no reason for data source consolidation. We will leave everything where it is, cherry pick and replicate the attributes and data we want into a centralized CMDB record and make sure they are up-to-date through reconciliation.

3) CMDB federation is the dynamic, spontaneous creation of a CI view from different existing data sources.

The 'CMDB data' already exists in the myriad of data sources and there is no need to create a central record – we just need to pull it all together in a virtual data warehouse model to create a current view of the existing data sources. In this approach, a central record is never created.

■ 6.2 Application 1: CMDB federation is the exception, not the rule

This approach starts with a belief in four core truths:

1. The CMDB is the central repository of record for all IT assets.
2. The CMDB is the singular trusted source of data and is used by all IT management disciplines and not just ITIL processes.
3. Federation to other databases applies only when the child data is residing in an IT tool or application database that has unique functionality and the source can be trusted as accurate and under control.
4. A best practice of data management is that you only store and manage it once if at all possible.

The outcome of these four truths or principles implies that there is an overall goal to *consolidate* all of the IT data management sources (regardless of who manages them) into one master source when those sources are '<u>like</u>', meaning that they have the same basic purpose (ie store data about CIs).

Additional Consideration: The number of attributes stored in a source database being evaluated for consolidation does not qualify as a basis for unique functionality. A decision on how many attributes should be managed in the CMDB should represent the <u>balanced</u> interest of all stakeholders interested in the data. This includes the owners of the original source database as well as the other groups and processes that require access to it. The final decision about what attributes will be managed at a controlled or un-controlled level is a deliverable of the CMDB data modeling step of the project.

All of these like-data sources, be they spreadsheets or enterprise database solutions, are candidates for consolidation into one source, the central CMDB. And yes, by consolidation, we mean elimination of the original database in favor of the central one. Remember the principle of managing data only once.

However, there are many sources of data that have unique functionality. For example; data stored in active directory which is used for rights management, a systems management tool used for discovery or event correlation, or a financial management application used for costing and billing.

Good examples of federation include:

1. When we look at a CI record and examine the financial attributes we are actually looking at data stored in the enterprise resource planning (ERP) application.
2. When we look at the hardware attributes, these are sourced from a discovery tool where we have selected only 12 attributes for the CI record out of potentially hundreds that are discoverable from the existing source.
3. People and organizational data comes from active directory, the HR tool or the email global address list.

Each of these examples represent a source of data with a unique functionality which is above and beyond the goal of managing data about CIs, and represents an excellent candidate for federation rather than consolidation.

While it is generally considered a best practice to manage data once, it is not always possible to avoid data replication. Often for technical or security reasons it is not possible or desirable to provide a real time view into the child data source; therefore, it is essential to have the capability to perform a regular reconciliation of the two sources through an automated means.

6.2.1 Three traditional objections to this view of federation

1. The ITSM processes do not need all of that data, so why should we confuse the CMDB with information that these processes do not require?
2. The database would be huge and performance would be an issue.
3. The cost of this consolidation would outweigh the benefit.

The first argument assumes that having a source of record where we track all relevant CIs in relationship to each other and IT services is only of use to the processes focused on Service Management. This is simply not true – procurement, software configuration, audit, security architecture and engineering, and project management to name a few also have a use for the CMDB.

The second argument is not well-founded since it is unclear as to how many CIs we are actually talking about managing. Many organizations by the definition of an asset deem certain CIs not worthy of management simply due to their relative financial cost (ie keyboards or perhaps monitors). Larger organizations can get into the double and maybe triple digit thousands, but that would be the outside number and this is well within the capability of the enterprise database solutions in use today.

The primary reason why an organization has multiple solutions for managing data is a result of history, politics and IT procurement practices focused at the domains. Based on a traditional technology management view, each IT domain is managed as a unique function and procures tools for its own needs (eg the database group has a database on databases, the server group has one database for Unix boxes and another for Wintel machines, the application groups track their applications, the network group is just concerned with network components, etc.). From this perspective, each group has built separate data sources to manage their own CIs.

Unless an IT organization can understand how any technology component connects to another and how they both impact a business process, it is very difficult to claim alignment with business objectives. What do you do when you realize that managing each domain in mythical isolation prohibits you from understanding the relationship of dependency between them? It is only when an organization begins to move to a service orientation that this question becomes a burning issue. This paradigm shift requires the creation of a CMDB where CIs can be modeled in relation to each other. Even more important is how the CIs are bundled to create systems that in turn support IT Services as consumed by the business.

Once upon a time the business had separate applications to support business processes such accounts receivable, inventory management, procurement, payroll, etc. Each of them had their own separate databases on different platforms which needed to be connected through complex integrations. However, IT stepped up to the plate and said that it would make more sense to have a suite of connected applications all getting their data from the same primary central source with federation to other internal and external sources applied when necessary.

The Enterprise Resource Planning (ERP) Suite was born.

If we preach this as a good strategy for the business, what makes IT any different? The answer, of course, is that we are not – instead, we are only a few years earlier in the management maturity curve.

The follow-on question then becomes why keep two tools to maintain data about the same CIs? Unless there is some significant functionality difference the choice – not to consolidate these duplicate sources of CI data at some point in the near future - is based on politics and emotion, not logic and cost.

The final argument assumes that managing data once in a single repository is somehow more expensive than managing and supporting multiple redundant data sources and tools. It would be a very interesting exercise to do a total cost of ownership assessment on the various tools in the organization today and compare it to a centralized solution. For many organizations this model would represent significant consolidation savings through the removal of redundant tools, streamlining the associated management processes and a reduction in the resources required to support them.

Each time an organization buys hardware, and installs, supports and buys licenses and maintenance contracts for data management solutions, it incurs an initial and ongoing cost. To consolidate even a third of these could represent significant long term savings.

To be fair, for some organizations many of the current data sources are low tech and have limited overhead costs. It is difficult to suggest that doing away with the spreadsheets in favor of an enterprise CMDB would save money based on consolidation: however it is a true statement that maintaining both the spreadsheet and the central CMDB is not an efficient use of resources. Add to this the cost of developing complex integrations that are not required and the third argument is hard to justify.

6.3 Application 2: CMDB federation is the rule, not the exception

The second application of the term federation is the reverse of the previous one. This use assumes a premise that the CMDB is used only by ITIL processes. Thus, it also largely presumes that there is limited value in trying to remove redundant data management tools in the IT organization.

In this model, the siloed IT functions graciously permit 'their' respective data sources to be tapped into by the central CMDB for which they feel limited by no personal accountability. In this model the CMDB is tolerated as required to support management processes like Change and Incident instead of being considered the central repository of record for general IT management.

In concept what is being suggested in this model is the creation of an instantiated data warehouse where source data is drawn to a central record that gathers history over time.

A data warehouse is a database geared towards the business intelligence requirements of an organization. The data warehouse integrates data from the various operational systems and is typically loaded from these systems at regular intervals. Data warehouses contain historical information that enables analysis of business performance over time.

There is a primary cultural difference between ITIL Configuration Management and distributed inventory management. Distributed inventory management represents a principle that each group updates their data in accordance with their personal need and culture. For some groups like the Unix Admins, this might be a daily activity, but for others it could be weekly, quarterly or based on best effort.

ITIL Configuration Management on the other hand requires almost real time accuracy in order to be trusted to the point where people will use this data for various processes and management decision-making.

Given that, the challenge with this second approach to federation is that it is very difficult to enforce data update and management at the source. If there are challenges with the controls managing the original source database, the owners of an ITIL-focused CMDB are out of luck and they have little to say about it ('you get what you get, and be thankful you get it').

In addition, the management overhead with this approach is much higher than the previous model. Every CI added to the environment always needs to be added to both the source database and the central CMDB, with the additional effort of establishing the link and reconciliation rules between the two sources.

Please consider that many organizations have a high volume of new CIs added to the environment on a regular basis. The creation of a backlog and the possibility of failure based on relational and technical complexities are exponentially higher with this model. Many organizations begin with this approach since it is the politically easier of the two models, but they have to re-start their project (with the associated cost implications) using Application #1: Federation as the exception, not the rule.

■ 6.4 Application 3: The dynamic view from existing distributed data

The third definition of federation is much like the one just addressed, and it struggles with many of the same challenges. However, in this application a central CI record is not actually created; instead, this model is based on the concept of creating a dynamic on-demand compilation of a view from existing distributed data each time that a request is made.

This model is a sometimes referred to as a Virtual Data Warehouse:

An enterprise data warehouse constructed of multiple data marts and a request broker computer application. The data warehouse does not physically exist except through out the formation of the integrated data marts.

Source: University of Southern California

While this solves the problem of creating two sources for managing the same data, it comes with another inherent challenge. In the ITSM community, it is considered best practice not only to create relationships between CI records, but also relationships from CI records to process records.

For example, the following relationships are critical to support ITSM:

- the ability to associate CI records to each other to model systems and services as consumed by the business
- the ability to associate Incident, Problem, Change and Release records to CIs throughout their lifecycle
- the ability to associate specific SLAs and business rules to CI records

When the CI is not instantiated and is only a virtual view on distributed data sources, these CI-to-process relationships become severely restricted, if not impossible.

■ 6.5 Summary

A key benefit of adopting a best practice standard is the adoption of a common language. This is, without a doubt, one of the things many organizations find attractive about ITIL; however, consider that the term 'federation' is used by many in regard to implementing the CMDB, but has three separate applications depending on whom you are talking with.

The next time this topic comes up, it would be wise to conduct a definition check as to which one of the three applications is meant.

To help you assess the right approach for your organization, you should:

1. review all current repositories and data sources
2. determine if these sources are 'unique'
3. define the long-term CMDB scope to include all data sources that are not considered unique or are not in a controlled state (this can be phased over time)
4. identify owners of these data sources and include them in the overall CMDB planning and design initiative
5. document and socialize the planned federation approach agreed to by the design team
6. develop an object model that incorporates this approach and the required attributes and relationships that will add value to your CMDB

Creating a federated data model is a necessity for the successful implementation of a CMDB strategy; however, the approach you use can make a difference between long term success and failure. By experience, we find the first approach listed in this chapter is by far the most successful over the long term, even though it is harder politically to initiate and achieve without a clear vision and definitive executive support.

Data source consolidation and centralization is the rule, and federation is applied only when a business case for unique functionally has been established.

7

Developing A Quality Driven
Measurement Framework

The purpose of this chapter is to describe an approach for how IT can measure performance through metrics that are designed to facilitate decision-making, and improve performance and accountability through collection, analysis and reporting. This global practice applies to all of IT/IT Division/Departments.

7.1 Measuring Process

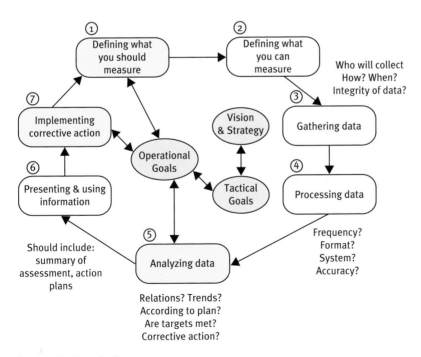

Figure 7.1: The Measuring Process

Measurement is an activity used to identify and perform data gathering. In order to make use of this data, one needs to create a measurement process (ie a set of activities designed to move from simple data gathering through to information assessment, to produce knowledge and understanding of the infrastructure that is being managed).

Organizations will realize a greater probability for success if they adopt the following guidelines in the development of metrics, whether for the entire enterprise or for departmental or individual performance plans:

1. **Define What You Should Measure**

   Based on the goals of the target audience (Operational, Tactical or Strategic), a Process Owner needs to define what should be measured in a perfect world. To do this, map the activities of the process you need to measure. Then, consider what measurements would indicate that each activity is being performed consistently and can determine the health of the process.

2. **Define What You Can Measure**

   Identify the measurements you can provide based on existing tool sets, organizational culture and process maturity. Note there may be a gap in what you can measure versus what you should measure. Quantify the cost and business risk of this gap to validate any expenditures for tools.

3. **Gathering The Data**

   Gathering concentrates on collecting the raw data required for monitoring and measuring IT services and components. Gathering the data is a repetitive set of tasks. Consider automation, or assign the tasks to gather the data to the appropriate roles in your organization. You should ensure that you have the correct data collection methodology in place.

4. **Processing The Data**

   Once you have gathered the data, the next step is to process the data into the required format. This step begins the transformation of raw data into packaged information. Use the information to develop insight into the performance of your process. Exceptions and alerts need to be considered at this step, as they can serve as early indicators that processes are breaking down. Process the data into information (ie creating logical groupings which allow you to perform step 5).

5. **Analyzing The Data**

   Data Analysis transforms the information into knowledge of the events that are affecting the organization:

   - Are there any trends?
   - Are changes required?
   - Are we operating according to plan?

- Are we meeting targets?
- Are corrective actions required?

6. **Presenting and using the Information**
   Considering the target audience, make sure that you identify exceptions to the process and benefits that have been revealed or can be expected. Data gathering occurs at the fourth level of an organization. Format this data into knowledge that all levels can appreciate and gain insight into their needs and expectations. This can be done by way of:

   - reports
   - monitors
   - action plans
   - evaluations
   - recommendations

7. **Implementing Corrective Action**
   Use the knowledge gained to optimize, improve and correct processes. Managers need to identify issues and present solutions. With this activity, link back to the goals of your audience; explain how the corrective actions to be taken will improve performance.

7.2 Risks

Many metrics end up being used because they are easy to measure, not because they measure meaningful information. Often, organizations mistakenly fail to define what they should measure and also fail to execute on analysis and implementing corrective action.

Failure to define what should be measured will result in metrics that are not aligned to the organizational goals and strategies. Bad metrics can drive dysfunctional behavior that can set an organization in the wrong direction.

Without analysis of the metrics, what you end with is nothing more than a string of numbers showing metrics that are meaningless. It is not enough to simply look at this month's figures and accept them without question, even if they meet SLA targets. You should analyze the figures to stay ahead of the game. Without analysis, you merely have information; with analysis, you have knowledge. If you find anomalies or poor results, then you have an opportunity to improve.

7.3 Requirements

Each Process Owner will follow a consistent approach for reporting their key performance areas in a means that is understandable, relevant and actionable – and supports a proactive and measurable approach to continuous improvement. This can be achieved by:

- clearly defined links between operational, tactical and strategic level goals and measurements
- clearly defined Corporate and IT goals
- identification of CSFs to support the overarching goals of IT and the Business
- development of KPIs and Key Goal Indicators (KGIs) to support the CSFs selected by IT and the Business

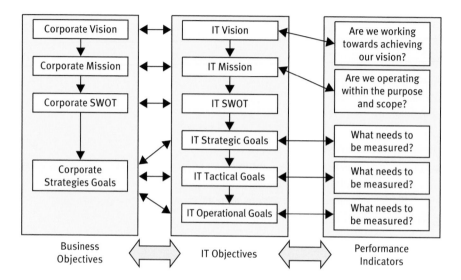

Figure 7.2: Business Perspective on IT

In developing business plans and conducting strategic planning and goal setting, some very basic questions needs to be addressed:

- What is our vision statement and where do we want to be?
- What is our mission or why do we exist as an organization?
- Where are we now? *SWOT analysis*
- How can we get there? *Business plans*
- What would tell us if we arrived? *Metrics*

Guidance documents include the vision statement and mission statements. With values, vision and mission understood, a strategy should be developed. Details of how to live the mission statement and reach the vision are captured in the specific business plans. Develop goals using the SMART test:

S - specific: clear and focused to avoid misinterpretation
M - measurable: can be quantified and compared to other data
A - attainable: achievable, reasonable, and credible under conditions expected
R - realistic: fits into the organization's constraints and is cost effective
T - timely: doable within the time frame given

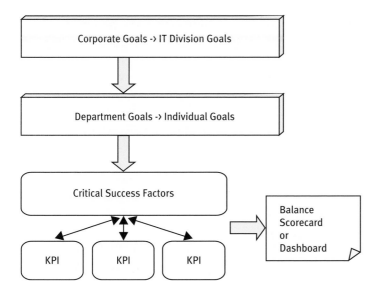

Figure 7.3: Goals and Objectives

■ 7.4 Rationale For Measurement

We measure to:

- validate what we do and how we are helping meet organizational goals and objectives
- justify the need for resources, technology to meet organizational goals and objectives
- direct actions to be taken when appropriate
- intervene when processes are not working the way they are supposed to

The business perspective of measuring IT:

- ability of IT services to meet business needs
- business satisfaction with IT service provision
- business benefits in the areas of productivity, effectiveness, efficiency and economy
- financial issues: Understanding cost of IT service, control of IT costs, accountability of IT costs to the business
- quality of IT service provision and support of IT use
- communication between the business and IT, and degree of mutual understanding
- degree to which business understands the management of IT infrastructure and IT service provision

7.4.1 Balanced Scorecard

The development and communication of a balanced scorecard is the responsibility of the IT Management Team. First introduced in 1990s, BSC is an aid to organizational performance management. It helps to target not only on financial targets, but also internal processes, customers, innovation/learning organizational issues. The BSC is a conceptual framework for translating an organization's vision into a set of performance indicators distributed among four perspectives: Financial, Customer, Internal Business Processes, and Learning and Growth.

Indicators are maintained to measure an organization's progress toward achieving its vision; other indicators are maintained to measure the long term drivers of success. Through the BSC, an organization monitors both its current performance (finances, customer satisfaction, and business process results) and its efforts to improve processes, motivate and educate employees, and enhance information systems. These are comprehensive measures that can directly relate the value of IT to corporate performance metrics.

BSC is not a typical IT principle; nevertheless, it is complementary to ITIL. When implemented within IT, it provides a means to measure the performance of the IT organization. BSC proposes that department goals, targets and metrics need to be developed for the following areas to truly understand the health of an organization:

- Customer: How do customers see us?
- Internal: What must we excel at?
- Innovation: Where can we improve and create new value?
- Financial: How do we improve cost efficiency?

Of the four perspectives, three deal with the future. Financial is the only perspective that looks at the past.

7.4.2 Links to ITIL

- Customer perspective: discussed in Service Level Management process and formulated within the SLA
- Internal Processes: all Service Support and Service Delivery Processes
- Financial: budgeting, Cost Management (how hosts are allocated to the customer), Chargeback (how customers pay for the services rendered)
- Learning and Growth: refers to staffing training and investing in hardware/software and projects

7.4.3 Management Reporting and KPIs

To govern or manage any information-based process, it is necessary to establish a variety of reports and metrics to understand how the process is being executed. The Process Owner and management team will need to choose KPIs to provide information on the health and relative maturity of the process. KPIs measure progress toward goals as reflected in CSFs; KPIs are then quantifiable measurements, or metrics.

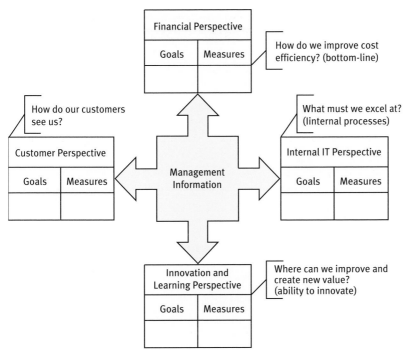

Figure 7.4: Links to ITIL

- KPI Categories:

    - Compliance: Are we doing it?
    - Quality: How well are we doing it?
    - Performance: How fast or slow are we doing it?
    - Value: Is what we are doing making a difference?

A single measure may contain or cover more than one category. This in itself is not an issue; understand that when this occurs, the success criterion for this measure is more difficult to satisfy.

7.4.4 Choosing The KPIs

Ideally, to measure a process at least one KPI per category should be chosen to provide a balanced perspective; however, due to the difficulty of measurement or tool limitation, process management staff may find it necessary to limit what is measured according to what category is the most important to the objective of the process.

1. establish the core objective of the process
2. evaluate which category is of the highest priority to achieve the process objective
3. define measures according to the categories which are appropriate to achieve the overall process objective

In order to select which KPIs are most suited to provide a health and maturity reading, a framework for measurement identification will be employed.

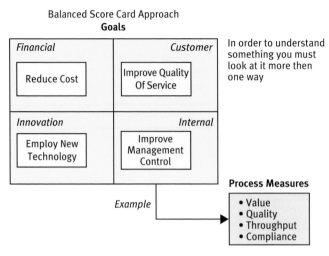

Figure 7.5: Measurement Framework

The Measured Framework diagram represents a dashboard by which the Process Owner can determine the health of a process. A minimum of one or two measurements should be determined for each quadrant to ensure a balanced perspective on the use and effectiveness of the process.

1. Value: reports or surveys to measure the effectiveness and perceived value of the process to the stakeholders and users
2. Quality: process quality indicators are typically activity-based and are established to measure the quality of individual or key activities as they relate to the objective of the end-to-end process
3. Performance: metrics established under this quadrant measure the average process throughput or cycle time (eg metrics to capture the speed and performance of the stated process objective and output)
4. Compliance: process compliance seeks to measure the percentage of process deployment across the IT organization; a process may have a good perceived value, good quality and speedy throughput, but only be adhered to by a fraction of the IT organization

7.4.5 Building A Measurement Grid

1. Define the measure.
2. Determine the KPI category.
3. Establish the policy and target (target will change with process maturity).
4. Determine the tool or medium to realize the report.

5. Define the output format (graph, data, etc.).
6. Define distribution list and report frequency.

Category	Measure	Policy	Target	Tool
Value, Quality	# of incidents resolved outside of SLA	All incidents to be resolved within SLA	90% of the time	Incident Module

Table 7.1: A Measurement Grid

7.5 Implementation Strategy

Implementation Steps:

1. Translating the vision (building consensus around the organizations vision and strategy). The strategic mission statements must be translated into tactical and operational objectives.
2. Inventory your performance reporting and assess the relevance of these reports to the business. Are they action-oriented? Are they linked to business performance and goals? Are they intelligible to a non-IT person?
3. Interview your Customers/Executives to understand what is relevant to them. Customer expectations will enable you to tailor the IT organization's contribution to business processes.
4. Create performance reports that are clear, concise and action-oriented by the business stakeholders that receive them.
5. Communicating and linking (communicating and setting goals, targets and metrics). Departmental, team, and individual goals, targets, and metrics must be directly linked to IT and Organizational goals.
6. Business Planning (applying measurement data to strategic plans). Measurement data should be used with modeling and forecasting for strategic planning and alignment with business objectives.
7. Feedback and learning (opportunity for strategic learning) provides a balanced and informed basis for decisions regarding possible infrastructure and resource adjustments in real time.

7.6 Translating A KPI Improvement To Productivity

When evaluating a KPI improvement for a productivity gain or cost reduction, one must determine the net gain by understanding how the improvement is offset by additional requirements for value add and non-value add work:

- **Value Add:** activity that directly results in achieving the goal of the process
- **Non-Value Add / Administration:** activity that is necessary, but is focused on tasks

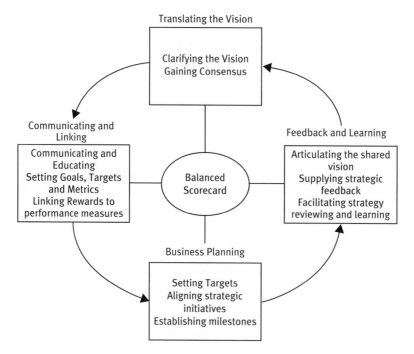

Figure 7.6: Implementation Steps

related to administration, governance or managerial activity that does not directly result in achieving the goal of the process
- **Waste Work:** activity that is redundant, not required or inefficient and does not support the goal of the process

A balanced approach to expressing an improvement gain from a productivity viewpoint would be to understand how the improvement translates into the following three categories:

- **Resources:** additional capacity and efficiency added to existing resources
- **Cost:** a reduction of cost in achieving the objective or goal of the process
- **Quality:** the positive or negative relationship of the first two factors on the quality of the delivery of the goal or objective

Measuring Intangibles to Tangible:

1. Can you identify what is being changed and why and what will be different?
2. Can the difference be observed? (Eg faster response time, increased revenue)
3. Can you measure the difference?
4. Can you compare it to the 'before state' or a benchmark?

KPI: # of repeat incidents reduced by 25%		
Goal: Increased Productivity measured by allocated time	Waste Work Removed	= -25%
Waste Removed = Reduced incidents	Value Added Work	= +10%
Value Added = Increased process activity	Non Value Add	= +5%
Non Value Add = Additional reporting effort	Net Improvement	= 10%

Table 7.2: Measuring Intangibles to Tangible

7.6.1 Productivity Approach

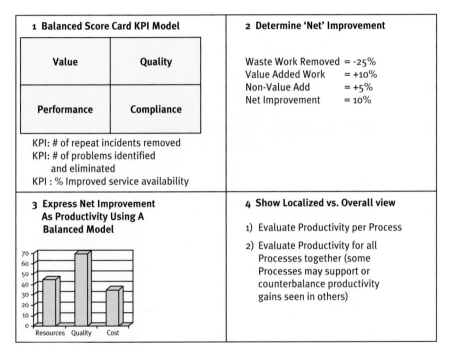

Figure 7.7: Productivity Approach

7.6.2 Service Desk Function

- Monthly overall performance, achievements and trend analysis
- telephony statistics such as number of inbound, outbound calls per agent, average talk time, average available time, per cent of abandoned calls, cost per call etc.
- reduced average time to live response
- reduced repetitive inquiries on solved issues
- increased user satisfaction with the effectiveness and efficiency of the help desk
- increased user confidence in the services of the help desk

Financial Goals	Performance Indicators	Customer Goals	Performance Indicators
Ability to control IT costs	– Accuracy of IT cost forecasts	Quality of IT services	– Availability of IT services (in IT users' perceptions)
Economy of IT	– Competitiveness of IT costs to the business	Reliability of IT services	– Compliance to SLAs; Number and severity of IT
			– Service disruptions
Value of IT	– Costs of IT used in value adding business activities versus costs of IT used in overhead activities	Performance of IT services	– On-time IT service delivery (defined by customer)
		Support of hands-on users	– Number of registered user complaints about IT
Innovation Goals	**Performance Indicators**	**Internal Goals**	**Performance Indicators**
Business productivity	– Improvements in business turnover ascribable to IT	Change control	– Percentage of first time right IT changes
	– Reduction in business costs ascribed to IT	Economy of IT	– Hours spent on IT matters by business managers vs. total
Service culture	– Number of business improvements initiated by or with help from IT	Value of IT	– Hours of IT use by business staff
Flexibility	– Average lead-time of successful IT implementation		– Number of reported security violations

Table 7.3: Example Metrics – KPIs

7.6.3 Incident Management

- total number of incidents by phone, email, walk-in, etc.
- average elapsed time to resolve incidents
- percentage within promised response time
- cost per incident (need to be careful about this)
- percentage closed by Service Desk on first contact
- incidents per agent
- incidents per business unit/department, etc.

- incidents by category
- incidents by priority
- aged ticket analysis

7.6.4 Problem Management

- percentage of incidents defined as problems
- number of problems and errors, split by: status, service, impact, category, user group
- number and impact of incidents occurring before the root problem is closed or a known error is confirmed
- number of workarounds or temporary solutions provided
- number of RFCs issued
- resolution times with respect to service level requirements
- number of problems outstanding and expected resolution time

7.6.5 Change Management

- total number of RFCs raised (trends)
- number of changes by item, type, service, etc.
- breakdown of reasons for change
- percentage of urgent changes
- number of successful changes
- number of changes backed out
- number of incidents traced to changes
- number of changes that did not follow the process
- size of review and implementation backlog by item/priority
- number of incidents/problems reduced as a result of change

7.6.6 Configuration Management

- frequency and number of CMDB errors
- number of new CIs
- incidents and problems by CI
- frequency of unregistered CIs
- number and severity of breaches in SLAs caused by inaccurate CMDB information
- frequency and impact of incidents affecting the CMDB system
- number of occasions where distributed and remote software is at the wrong level
- frequency and duration of bottlenecks
- timeliness of management reports
- ability to cope with growth

7.6.7 Release Management

Number of:

- major and minor releases per reporting period
- builds/distributions aborted during process
- failed or backed out implementations plus builds rolled back after implementation
- software builds from sources other than the DSL
- unlicensed/unauthorized versions detected
- times the DSL is out of step with the CMDB
- detected viruses within the organization
- incidents/problems raised attributed to a release
- percentage of:
  - urgent releases
  - installations completed within agreed timescale
  - resource costs per release

7.6.8 Service Level Management

A Service Level Agreement (SLA) is a mutually agreed on contract between the service provider and the customer; therefore, it is an objective measure of performance. If only one metric is reported, then it should be on meeting SLA terms.

- how many SLAs/OLAs/UC are in place
- new SLAs, OLAs, UCs negotiated and agreed to
- number of reviewed and extended or renegotiated SLAs, OLAs, UCs
- regular reports are being generated
- reports generate action/discussion
- regular review meetings and any service improvement programs
- number of service breaches
- customer perception improving?

7.6.9 Availability Management

- agreed service hours, per service
- total down time per service
- detection elapsed time per incident
- response times per incident
- time taken to repair per incident
- actual availability compared with SLA requirements
- reliability – compared to expectations
- maintainability – compared to expectations
- serviceability – supplier performance compared with contractual conditions
- availability plan is modified as required

7.6.10 Capacity Management

- number of end-business processes suffering interruptions or outages caused by inadequate IT capacity and performance
- number of critical business processes not covered by a defined service availability plan
- percentage of critical IT resources with adequate capacity and performance capability, taking account of peak loads
- number of down-time incidents caused by insufficient capacity or processing performance
- percentage of capacity remaining at normal and peak loads
- time taken to resolve capacity problems
- percentage of unplanned upgrades compared with total number of upgrades
- frequency of capacity adjustments to meet changing demands

7.6.11 Service Continuity Management

- cost of:

    - loss of service or business
    - loss of revenue
    - loss of resources (staff, equipment, facilities)

- length of time to Recover from occurrence
- length of time before detection of impact of occurrence
- percentage of reduction to vulnerability (chance of repeat)
- cost of mitigating/preventive measure versus cost of recovery
- number and details of changes that require updates to the contingency plan
- percentage of test output meeting SLA requirements

7.6.12 Financial Management

- percentage of CIs with incorrect financial data
- percentage of cost predictions that are incorrect
- percentage of change management decisions where cost impact is omitted
- staff time spent on costing activities
- software/hardware overheads in collecting data for cost management
- percentage of variance between budgets, forecasts and actual costs
- percentage reduction in information service rates
- percentage increase in optimization of IT resources usage
- software license fees vs. available licenses

Process	KPI/Description	Type	Progress Indicator
Incident	Tickets resolved within target time	Value	Meets/exceeds target times.
Incident	% of Incidents closed – first call	Performance	Service Desk only – target is 80%.
Incident	Abandon Rate		Service Desk with ACD. 5% or less goal (after 24 seconds).
Incident	Count of Incident submitted by Support Group	Compliance	Consistency in number of incidents – investigation is warranted for 1) rapid increase which may indicate Infrastructure investigation; 2) rapid decrease which may indicate compliance issues.
Problem	% of repeated Problems over time	Quality	Problems that have been removed from the infrastructure and have re-occurred. Target: less than 1% over a 12 month rolling time frame.
Problem	% Root Cause with permanent fix	Quality	Calculated from Problem Ticket start date to permanent fix found. This may not include implementation of permanent fix. Internal Target: 90% of Problems – within 40 days; External Target: 80% of Problems – within 30 days; Internal = BMO internal; External = 3rd Party/vendor.
Problem	% and number of Incidents raised to Problem Management	Compliance	Sorted by Infrastructure (Internal and External) and Development (Internal and External).
Change	% of RFCs successfully implemented without back-out or issues	Quality	Grouped by Infrastructure / Development.
Change	% of RFCs that are emergencies	Performance	Sort by Infrastructure or Development – and by Emergency Quick fix (service down) or Business requirement.
Configuration	Number of CI additions or updates	Compliance	Configuration Item Additions or updates broken down by group – CMDB / Change Modules.
Configuration	Number of records related to CI	Performance	Number of associations grouped by process.
Release	% of Releases using exceptions	Value	Exceptions are criteria deemed mandatory – identify by groups.
Release	% of Releases by-passing process	Compliance	Identify groups by passing Release Process.

Process	KPI/Description	Type	Progress Indicator
Capacity	Action required	Value	Number of services that require action vs. total number of systems.
Capacity	Capacity related problems	Quality	Number of Problems caused by Capacity issues sorted by group.

Table 7.4: Example Dashboard of Key Performance Indicators

8 The Theory of Constraints and Continuous Service Improvement

8.1 Introduction

In his book, *The Goal*, Eli Goldratt presents his model on the Theory of Constraints (TOC), in the form of a novel where he identifies new measurements for the analysis of productivity and ultimately, profit. The core truth of the TOC is that every system or process has at least one constraint or bottleneck, and that the identification of this constraint should be the primary focus for any improvement activity.

The objective of this chapter is to examine the model for systems measurement and analysis that Goldratt developed, and then to apply it to intellectual or business processes. To achieve this objective, this chapter will expand on Goldratt's original concepts based on manufacturing systems, to cover IT business process and procedural issues.

Three core truths govern the application of TOC:

- A system or a process cannot be more efficient than its limiting factor, bottleneck or constraint.
- Every system or process has at least one constraint or bottleneck.
- In order to manage a constraint, it is first necessary to identify it.

8.2 Eli Goldratt's *The Goal*

In the storyline presented in *The Goal*, an infamous machine known as the NCX10 is eventually identified by the plant manager and hero of the book as the major constraint or bottleneck to the plants systems and processes. This knowledge ultimately helps the plant to determine where an increase in productivity and efficiency will lead to increased profits. The book is written in such a way that the reader cannot help but learn foundational truths whilst enjoying the engaging plot. However, the journey to this profound discovery is not straightforward: many false turns and starts are attempted before the core truths are uncovered and the results realized.

In the search for increased revenues, many improvements are made to various systems and activities, and while these improvements realized limited benefits for the area under scrutiny, mysteriously, they did not impact the overall goal of making more profit for the factory.

The basic premise that Goldratt explores in his book is that improvement initiatives must be focused on removing system or process constraints, not on individual activities or tasks. Typically, organizations will focus on a single dimension, like 'where does it hurt?', and focus improvements on that pain point. However, in many cases the identified point of improvement is actually symptomatic of the true constraint.

■ 8.3 How does TOC apply to continuous improvement?

The practical application of the TOC is that it effectively focuses the attention of the organization on the root cause as opposed to the symptoms. Goldratt states that there is really no choice in the matter: 'either you manage constraints or they manage you'. The measurement framework that he proposes is similar to the balanced scorecard principle of multi-dimensional or balance reporting.

TOC advocates that the organization take a three-dimensional and prioritized view of three core business concepts:

- inventory
- operating expense
- throughput

Although executives from financial management and manufacturing organizations are familiar with these terms, IT managers are less likely to develop scorecards or KPIs that track the relationship and interplay of these concepts. Even more challenging is the interpretation of these principles in terms of IT management processes.

To apply these traditional financial terms to IT Service Management, one needs to expand the definitions beyond their traditional concepts. In essence, you need to be able to map all the activity related to executing a system or IT business process in terms of one of these three factors. The following definitions are much broader in scope and represent a significant departure from traditional management accounting principles.

■ 8.4 TOC definitions

Inventory: includes all of the money, investment, outstanding issues, pending changes, unresolved incidents, excess capacity, etc. that an organization has tied up in an un-sellable, un-finished, un-resolved, undeliverable or pending state. Goldratt goes on to define that inventory can be broken down into:

- **pre-process inventory:** stuff that is currently waiting in queue in a raw or input state, that is to be handled or transformed by a system or process, ie calls that are waiting in the automatic call distributor (ACD) system or emails that have not been answered by the Service Desk
- **active inventory:** stuff that is currently within the system or process, and is currently being transformed into a desired or sellable output state, ie change records that are currently being assessed, authorized and scheduled
- **post-process inventory:** stuff that has been successfully transformed into a desired output, but has not been delivered to a client, sold, confirmed, resolved or generated profit, ie the Service Desk's feedback calls to the users to confirm that an incident, which has been resolved, can be permanently closed

In TOC, the concept of inventory is in disagreement with the conventional balance sheet definition of inventory as an 'asset' or a 'good thing' and redefines inventory to be essentially an undesirable liability. This is largely due to requisite operating expenses associated with carrying excessive amounts of each type of inventory.

- **Operating expense:** this includes all of the money, time, energy, thought, resource allocation, overtime, etc. tied up in the process of converting raw material or inventory into the end goal of the system or process. The observable fact is that increased inventory in any state requires a proportionate increase of operating expense to carry the increasing levels of inventory. Goldratt points out that a natural outcome of increased operating expense is the reduction of cash flow for the organization. However, in respect to business processes that deal with intangible inventory such as un-resolved incidents, cash flow can be translated into reduction of time or resource availability. As the process agents work on managing the increasing stockpile of each type of inventory, they have less time to work on other things and to meet service targets. The end result is that the higher the inventory levels within the process, the less time staff have to respond to new capital projects or even their department related functional activities.

Throughput: this can be defined as the rate or speed at which inventory is moved through the end-to-end system or process, and delivered to the customer in order to realize the **goal** of profit, resolution, deployment, etc. By increasing the rate of throughput, the inventory is reduced by moving it in, through and out of the process. By realizing the goal of the system or process, the organization realizes the coveted return on investment, which could mean cash in pocket or more time to work on other things.

Goldratt observes that these three core principles are inseparably linked and that a change, either positive or negative in any one of these three dimensions, will automatically result in a proportionate change in at least one, or maybe both, of the other two. For example, if actions are taken to reduce inventory, there will be a reflective reduction in the carrying costs (operating expense).

Saying this, one could assume that the ultimate goal of an improvement initiative is to optimize throughput, which in turn will reduce inventory level and lower operating expenses. These activities should also theoretically improve the cash flow situation and provide all concerned with a better quality of life.

However, senior management has traditionally emphasized reduction of operating expense first, followed by increasing throughput and finally, inventory reduction. According to Goldratt, the biggest gains are to be realized by first increasing throughput, then by reducing inventory. Operating expense reduction should occur as a natural result of the first two activities and should be seen as the third priority.

■ 8.5 Identifying constraints

The first task is to identify those illusive constraints. Goldratt uses the assembly line as an excellent example as to how to do this. The plant manager, through a series of measurements, was able to discover that widgets were piling up in front of the new 'state of the art' NCX10. The rate at which the products could be built and shipped was ultimately tied to the pace at which the machine released its inventory to the next step in the process.

The key here is to take a long view of the end-to-end process, and look for tell tale evidences of a bottleneck. To do this, an organization needs to look for a set of multiple mini processes, which in turn have inputs, activities and outputs. These mini processes will then pass on the post-process inventory to the next step or stage in the overall system. When the overall process is viewed in this way, one can begin to identify where inventory is piling up in a pre-process state due to a lack of adequate capacity in the downstream activity.

Goldratt's prognosis at this point is to add additional or alternative capacity in the system to remove the constraint. This bottleneck phenomenon is not unlike an accident scene on a highway where everyone slows down to look. This activity chokes the throughput in the system. After the accident scene is passed, the process speeds up immediately. However, unless you break several traffic laws you still arrive late at your destination, the damage has been done and the delay realized.

Question: What typically occurs when you remove a recognized bottleneck?
Answer: Another bottleneck appears somewhere else in the process.
Result: We have identified the next area of optimization to increase our throughput.

Using the traffic example, no sooner is the accident passed, than the traffic slows down once again due to a road construction site.

8.6 Where are constraints?

General principles that have been observed in the search for the illusive constraints are:

- The constraint can be internal or external to your organization
- The constraint can be tangible, like a piece of machinery or intangible like a policy or procedure
- 80% of the time the constraint will be intangible

Goldratt's process for identifying constraints is very similar to well-known quality models such as Dr. Deming's (Plan, Do, Check, Act) circle of continuous improvement:

1. identify the constraint
2. analyze and exploit the constraint
3. subordinate all other improvement activities to the necessity of removing the constraint
4. if, after steps 2 and 3, there are no tangible results, elevate or escalate the constraint until either additional or alternative capacity is applied to remove the constraint
5. find the next constraint

The core principle being defined by this five-step process is that TOC is all about continuously looking for the next bottleneck. The following list identifies several areas where organizations can typically find constraints:

- capacity constraints (resources, bandwidth, quality, performance)
- policy and measurement constraints
- wrong actions or lack of initiative
- authority constraints (responsibility without authority)
- sales constraints
- human relationship constraints (competition or negative relationships between people and departments)

This list of constraints is not definitive, but can help an organization begin to narrow down where and how improvements need to be made to increase the throughput of whatever system or process is under scrutiny.

In conclusion, Eli Goldratt's Theory of Constraints places a valuable and practical tool in the hands of individuals involved in activities that relate to the ongoing management of intellectual and business processes. To restate an earlier quote: 'there is really no choice in the matter, either you manage constraints or they manage you'.

9

Appendices

Appendix 1: An example of a Communications Plan Matrix

Target Group	Key Messages	Frequency	Mode/Channels	Responsible	Expected Results
Sponsors	Project Goals and Status	Monthly	email	Project Manager	Buy-in and commitment Feedback on revised processes
Steering Committee	Project Goals, Revised Processes and Procedures	Monthly	Status Meetings	Project Manager	Feedback on revised processes Support for process adherence
Process Team Owners	Deliverable Status Deliverable Quality	Weekly	Status Meetings	Project Manager	Feedback on revised processes
Core (Process) Team	Feedback on deliverables	Ongoing	email, Video and Teleconferences Status Meetings	Project Manager	Plan and design project deliverables
Project Stakeholders	Deliverables revised processes and procedures	Ongoing	email, Video and Teleconferences	Project Manager Project Team	Provide input and review of project deliverables Validation of new processes
IT Staff	Project Goals, Revised Processes and Procedures	Every 3 months	Quarterly Meetings Newsletters email Lunchtime forums	IT Directors and Managers	Feedback on revised processes Adherence to new processes

Target Group	Key Messages	Frequency	Mode/Channels	Responsible	Expected Results
Program Steering Committee	Project Status	Monthly	email Presentations	Project Manager Project Team Leads	Buy-in and commitment Feedback on revised processes Remediate issues
Program Manager	Project Status	Weekly	email Status report	Project Manager Project Team Leads	Alignment of deliverables across all other project teams Risk Mitigation
Business Units	Project Goals Revised Processes	Monthly	email Newsletters	Project Manager Steering Committee	Adherence to new processes

Appendix 2: An example of a Process Dashboard Template

This Month's Major Milestones	Next Steps	Target Date	Status (Green, Yellow, Red)
•	•		
•	•		
•	•		
•	•		

Issues That Require Action	Requested Action				
• None at this time					

Key Performance Indicators	Reasons for Results	Actions Required	Owner	Due Date
•	•			
•	•			
•	•			
•	•			
•	•			

Processes:		IT Service Management Processes					
Status:	Yellow						
Process Owner							
Program Manager:							
Month:							

Appendix 3: Detailed Project Roles

Role	Responsibilities
Steering Committee and Project Approval Role A decision-making forum for the lifetime of medium and large projects. Ideally, this group should contain a senior representative from each of the major stakeholders of the project.	• provides direction and counsel to project team • prioritizes business initiatives based upon adherence to strategic direction and projected ROI • funds initiatives and monitors ongoing project costs vs progress • considers and approves/rejects revised project budgets • has authority to terminate projects (*direction/cost*) • sets expectations, targets and success criteria for deliverables • formally manages project scope and funding • reviews and approves milestone deliverables • resolves escalated cross-functional, progress and problem-solving issues • allocates resources • has authority to recommend projects be terminated (*direction/cost*) • approves post-implementation review
Sponsor A member of the Senior Management team (*or designate*) with a vested interest in the project, who can commit the time to the project.	• defines and manages content of project scope • chairs the project Steering Committee • champions the initiative and is ultimately accountable for its success and benefit realization • is responsible of overall project communication plan and awareness campaign • makes business decisions and provides direction to the project team • ensures sustained buy-in of the project/initiative at management levels • ensures the project manager and team are kept informed of corporate strategies, other initiatives or changes that may impact the project • clarifies and communicates relevant business policies and guidelines • identifies project stakeholders/vested interests • ensures resolution of major issues • maintains current knowledge of the project (*project manager briefings, attends status meetings*) • authorizes spending of contingency budget • represents the project to the organization • has authority to recommend projects be terminated (*direction/cost*) • measures project deliverables against success criteria and ensures sustained adherence to schedule and budget commitments • provides regular feedback to team on performance versus expectations • chairs the post-implementation review and ensures results match original goal

Role	Responsibilities
Stakeholders Individuals or groups who may be impacted by the outcome of the project.	• identifies and communicates issues and concerns associated with the project in a clear, concise and timely manner to the project director/manager • serves as a liaison between the project team and their own functional area(s) by reviewing, commenting on and distributing project documents to all necessary parties • provides input for, or participates in the development stages of process and policy documents
Program Manager Required for complex projects, oversees the activities of Project Managers for specific elements of a large-scale program. Ensures alignment and integration of separate projects within the overall service improvement program.	• breaks down the program into logical components and packages these components into smaller projects • works with the sponsor and project managers, to establish an overall program organization structure, and delegates management of the projects to appropriately skilled resources • integrates project plans into an overall program plan and meets regularly with the project mangers to track status, issues, mitigation activities and risks • manages the overall program plan, updating and changing to reflect current scope, schedule and budget • works with Sponsor and Project Managers to plan the overall program charter, success criteria and deliverables • is responsible for the overall success of the service improvement program as measured by meeting the program success criteria developed by the steering committee • develops, gains approval for, and communicates the overall program goals, practices and business deliverables • anticipates problems and takes *(or recommends)* corrective action *(including recommendation to terminate)*; escalates issues and problems as necessary to sponsor and/or Steering committee • prepares and delivers regular overall project communication to relay progress and issues to all interested parties • manages expectations around activities and deliverables • ensures sustained buy-in at all levels • 'audits' projects to ensure adherence to established project practices and deliverable quality • identifies stakeholders/vested interests and ensures that they have a voice in the direction and progress of the project • manages scope change process, and updates the initiation document and program plan as necessary • manages formally issues and resolves conflicts • facilitates the negotiation with line managers for resources and/or deliverables

Role	Responsibilities
Project Manager Required for the management of small or medium projects.	*(The following points are applicable to a Project Manager who has been assigned responsibility for part of a larger project that is under the management of a Program Manager)* • develops Project Charter / Brief (as it relates to the sub-project) and high-level project plan (*deliverables, schedule, and budget*) • assists the Program Manager to identify stakeholders and vested interests • works with Sponsor, Program Manager and Process Owners, to define resource requirements, establish project organization structure and manage the project teams • anticipates problems and *takes (or recommends)* corrective action *(including recommendation to terminate)*; escalates issues and problems as necessary to the Program Manager and Steering Committee • creates detailed plan for the team (*based upon agreed time estimates*) • manages day-to-day project activities • works with the project team, to assign tasks, monitor and track progress (against the plan), and ensure acceptance of team deliverables • provides regular feedback to team members on delivery versus expectation
Process Owner The three major activities of the Process Owner are: Design, Coaching and Advocacy. Unlike other roles identified in this document the Process Owner role does not dissolve on the successful completion of the project, but continues as an ongoing resource requirement.	• is the primary process architect, who ensures that the process design is relevant and fit for purpose according to the defined project success criteria • coaches the process design team and stakeholders in understanding and implementing the process in the live environment • is the process champion and advocate of the process during the design period, and also undertakes the ongoing accountable role, ensuring the success and quality of the process as it applies to cross-functional organizational units • develops detailed project plans for their area of responsibility with team members and in consultation with project manager • validates task, effort and time estimates of team members • coaches team members to meet estimates and deliverables • identifies required resources • attends status meetings and reports on team progress • ensures quality of team deliverables • identifies gaps/issues and resolves issues • liaises with other teams as needed • reviews changes to business requirements • has a team building function • provides feedback on team member's performance

Role	Responsibilities
Strategic Process Advisor The role of the Strategic Process Advisor is responsible for assisting with scoping and defining the major project deliverables. In collaboration with the Client, Pink Process Consultant, and Project Manager.	• is responsible for knowledge transfer and the provision of timesaving tools and templates. The ultimate goal of the Process Advisor is to train internal resources with the skills and knowledge to continue ongoing process design and improvement activities • assists the Client, Process Consultant and Project Manager with scoping and resourcing of the process improvement projects. • provides guidance and knowledge around the integration of best practice frameworks and quality systems • leads onsite implementations often involving multiple internal process teams and Pink Consultants • assists with the high-level definition of project timelines and deliverables • participates in the review of major project milestones and contract negotiation • facilitates discussion of major scope changes to the project charter
Process Consultant The role of the Process Consultant is to provide knowledge, guidance and experience to the Sponsor, Steering Committee, Process Owners and Team Members to ensure quality and successful completion of the project deliverables.	• is responsible for knowledge transfer and the provision of timesaving tools and templates. The ultimate goal of the Process Advisor is to train internal resources with the skills and knowledge to continue ongoing process design and improvement activities • assists the Process Owner and Project Manager to develop detailed work breakdown structures and project plans based on templates and examples • assists the Process Owner and Project Manager in estimating work effort for activities and project tasks • ensures clear understanding of assigned tasks and defined deliverables • develops and conducts custom workshops to address the ongoing knowledge transfer requirements for the key deliverables defined by the scope statement of the project charter • ensures that the process development team does not expend resources and effort in time wasting activities and directions • assists the process team in the development of technology and automation requirements and advises on the selection and configuration of tools to underpin the process designs • is available to assist team on an 'as-required' basis • keeps up-to-date on team progress and communications • actively contributes to project success, making suggestions and providing consulting advice where appropriate

Role	Responsibilities
Core Process Team Member and Process Analysts Ideally, process team members are resourced from stakeholder groups of the new process. This is typically a temporary role defined by the lifecycle of the process improvement project. The process team members are directly responsible for the creation and generation of project deliverables. If required Pink Elephant can provide Process Analysts resources to fulfill this role.	• completes assigned tasks on time, within estimate and with specified quality • creates initial project deliverables in co-operation with other core team members • ensures clear understanding of assigned tasks and estimates effort and timeline for assigned deliverables • reports potential delays promptly and presents alternative plans for avoiding or recovering from them • attends all status and directional meetings (as required) • supports project manager in gaining and retaining buy-in and support from line managers and stakeholders • communicates regularly with stakeholders and provides opportunities for their input as it relates to assigned deliverables • actively contributes to the project's success
Extended Stake Holder Groups and Subject Matter Experts In order to maintain a control on cost but yet handle the political requirements for feedback, expertise, and sign off, additional stakeholder and subject matter experts will be defined and brought into the project at key times. The project work validation and feedback activities assigned to these individuals should not require significant changes in the volume of daily workload, but will add time to the duration of the project.	• reviews deliverables and provide timely feedback during the project lifecycle • provides guidance on improvements and modifications • provides technical and business related advice • assists with the awareness activities within their functional groups • assists with user acceptance testing of automated solutions • assists with the implementation of the processes • assists with ongoing continuous improvement activities

Appendix 4 Bibliography

OGC Service Support ITIL modules: Help Desk, Service Level Management, Understanding and Improving, ITIL Service Support

New Developments In Re-Engineering Organizations, Stephen Campell and Brian H. Kleiner

Leading Change, John P. Kotter, Harvard Business School Press, 1996

Various internal Pink Elephant consulting documents

Quality Management for IT Services, CCTA ITIL

The Goal, Eli Goldratt, North River Press, 1984

Business Service Management In 200, TechRepublic, June 2005, available at www.techrepublic.com

ITIL's Final Breakthrough: From 'What' to 'How', T. Mendel, Forrester Research, available at www2.cio.com/analyst/report2843.html

American ITIL: Best Practices Win Converts, NetworkWorld, August 3, 2004, available at www.networkworld.com/news/2004/083004itil.html

An Introductory Overview Of ITIL itSMF, April 2004, available at www.itsmfusa.org

Board Briefing On IT Governance, Information Systems Audit and Control Foundation, 2001, available at www.ITgovernance.org

Appendix 5: Definitions

ACD	Automatic Call Distributor (system)
AICPA	American Institute of Certified Public Accountants
ASL	Application Services Library: A library initiated by the Dutch Ministry of Defense
AS 8000	International standard for Corporate Governance
ATLAS™	Pink Elephant's secure, web-enabled knowledge management system
BCP	Business Continuity Plan
BSI	British Standards Institution
CI	Configuration Item
CIO	Chief Information Officer
CMDB	Configuration Management Database
CMM	Capability Maturity Model
COBIT	Control Objectives for Information and Related Technology
COSO	Committee of Sponsoring Organizations of the Treadway Commission
CSF	Critical Success Factor
Data Warehouse	A database geared towards the business intelligence requirements of an organization
DBA	Database Administrator
ERP	Enterprise Resource Planning
ETOM	Electronic Telecommunications Map
FCR	First Call Resolution
HD	Help Desk
ICT	Information and Communications Technology
ISACA	Information Systems Audit and Control Association
ITGI	IT Governance Institute
ITIL®	IT Infrastructure Library
ITSM	IT Service Management
ISO 9001:2000	International standard for Quality Management Systems
ISO 17799	International standard for IT Security Systems
ISO 20000	International standard for IT Service Management
JIT	Just In Time: An inventory system that reduces storage of materials or supplies
KGI	Key Goal Indicator
KPI	Key Performance Indicator
LAN	Local Area Network
MSP	Managed Service Providers
OGC	UK Office of Government Commerce
OLA	Operational Level Agreement
PID	Project Initiation Document

PIR	Post Implementation Review
PMI	Project Management Institute: Usually refers to their own established project management methodology
PMO	Project Management Office
PRINCE2™	*PRojects IN* Controlled *En*vironments: A project management methodology, covering the management, control and organization of a project
QMS	Quality Management System
RACI Matrix	An authority matrix, used within organizations to indicate roles and responsibilities
RFC	Request For Change
RFP	Request For Proposal
ROI	Return On Investment
Service Catalog	Defined by ITIL as a list of services that an organization provides
Six Sigma	Quality improvement methodology focused on the reduction of variation in all work processes
SLA	Service Level Agreement
SLM	Service Level Management
SPOC	Single Point Of Contact (for customers)
SOX	Sarbanes-Oxley: US federal Act of 2002, focused on ensuring internal controls relating to financial reporting and accounting
SOX Institute	Training and certification organization in line with SOX compliance and best practice
SAS-70	International auditing standard - AICPA Statement on Auditing Standards No. 70, *Service Organizations*
TOC	Theory Of Constraints
UC	Underpinning Contract

Appendix 6: About Pink Elephant

Service Lines

Pink Elephant's service lines each provide different, but complementary business solutions:

Business Process Consulting: Using the ITIL best practices approach as a springboard, Pink Elephant provides end-to-end solutions – from assessments, to strategic planning to implementation, continuous improvement and beyond. Experienced consultants work hand-in-hand with customers every step of the way.

Conferences and Special Events: Pink Elephant is the world's largest producer of IT Service Management conferences and delivers several major events per year to thousands of IT professionals.

Education: Pink Elephant is the most prolific creator and widespread distributor of ITIL training, and leads the way with education based ITIL V3's service lifecycle approach. Pink Elephant is internationally accredited by independent examination institutes that manage the ITIL certification program and is a Registered Education Provider with the Project Management Institute (PMI).

ATLAS™: ATLAS is a secure, web-enabled knowledge management system containing over 1,000 ITIL process deployment documents, including road maps, templates, RACI matrices, etc., ready and waiting for users to access, copy, customize and re-use.

ITIL Leadership

Pink Elephant has grown to become recognized globally as *The ITIL Experts* and is very proud of its commitment to the ITIL best practice framework. In fact, Pink Elephant has been involved in the "ITIL project" since its inception in 1987. Furthermore, Pink Elephant:

- Contributed to the ITIL V3 project (published in 2007):
  - Author of the Continual Service Improvement core volume
  - Member of ITIL V3's international exam qualification panel
- Developed new courses and public information sessions based on ITIL V3's service lifecycle:
  - ITIL V3 Foundations
  - Introduction To The ITSM Operations Process Model
- Supported the development of ITIL V2's core books (published in 2000):
  - Service Support (English and French editions)
  - Service Delivery (English and French editions)
- Promoted IT Service Management best practices internationally through podcasts, white papers, blogs, articles in IT publications and in presentations at international IT events

- Introduced ITIL to companies across a wide variety of industries, sizes, technical platforms and corporate cultures
- Created the International IT Service Management Conference and Exhibition, one of the largest events worldwide solely dedicated to ITIL
- Launched PinkVerify™, the only independent certification program worldwide that recognizes software that supports specific IT management processes
- Facilitated plans for an ITIL examination centre in North America (Loyalist College in Belleville, Ontario, Canada)
- First offered the Foundation, Practitioner and Management ITIL certification levels publicly in North America
- Launched a worldwide Foundations course in Control Objectives for Information and Related Technology (COBIT®), a framework that is complementary to ITIL for managing IT services and meeting legislative compliance
- Was a founding member of the IT Service Management Forum (now *it*SMF) – the worldwide networking group for IT Service Management professionals

Awards

Pink Elephant is recognized as a progressive and successful company and is the recipient of the following awards that reflect its corporate leadership excellence and business results:

- EXIN Award: Given to the organization with outstanding achievements in promoting the IT Service Management framework outlined in the IT Infrastructure Library (ITIL) – the world's most popular set of IT management best practices
- Top 100 Fastest Growing Companies in Canada – Awarded annually by PROFIT Magazine. Pink Elephant was recognized as one of Canada's fastest-growing companies (based on a comparison of revenue growth for five consecutive years)
- Top 100 Canadian IT Professional Services Organizations – Awarded by Branham300
- Top 100 Woman Entrepreneurs – 2001 – 2006: Awarded to Pink Elephant CEO, Fatima Cabral, by PROFIT magazine
- Ontario Global Traders Award – 2005: Awarded by the Ontario Government for achievements in innovation, leadership, product excellence and expansion into new markets